Green Tree Pythons As Pets.

Green Tree Python Comprehensive Owner's Guide.

Green Tree Python care, behavior, enclosures, feeding, health, myths and interaction all included.

by

Marvin Murkett and Ben Team

Table of Contents

About The Authors

Marvin Murkett is an experienced writer and a true animal lover. He has been keeping reptiles and amphibians for over 30 years. He enjoys writing animal books and advising others how to take care of their animals to give them a happy home.

Ben Team is an environmental educator and author with over 16 years of professional reptile-keeping experience. Ben has kept and bred reptiles for his entire adult life. He is an International Society of Arboriculture certified arborist, and he is state-licensed to perform nuisance wildlife removal.
Ben currently maintains www.FootstepsInTheForest.com, where he shares information, narration and observations of the flora, fauna and habitats of Metro Atlanta.

Foreword

Different snake species exhibit different foraging ecologies.

Some species, such as the infamous black mamba (*Dendroaspis polylepis*), actively search for food. They are generally fast, nimble and active snakes that may prowl with their heads held high off the ground. These snakes are often diurnal, and they overcome their relatively small prey via powerful venom or brute force. They often consume several food items in a short period of time, and they tend to eat relatively often.

At the other end of the spectrum, some snakes are ambush hunters that wait patiently for prey to come to them. Many of these snakes grow quite large, such as the anacondas (*Eunectes* sp.) of the Amazon rainforest, who lie patiently in the submerged vegetation, or African rock pythons (*Python sebae*) who lurk in the tall grass of the African savannah.

Whereas active snakes tend to be long and lithe, ambush hunters often have stout builds. Ambush hunters usually constrict their food or use powerful venom to subdue their prey. Many are intricately colored and patterned so that they camouflage well with their natural surroundings. These snakes eat relatively large, infrequent meals. They are rarely fast, and if threatened, they are more likely to stand their ground than active snakes are.

While North American and European snake enthusiasts live alongside a few ambush-hunting serpents, such as copperheads (*Agkistrodon contortrix*) and adders (*Vipera berus*), the zenith of this strategy occurs in far off rainforests, in the form of a relatively small python that lives in the trees.

Most aspects of green tree pythons (*Morelia viridis*) relate to their ambush hunting style. Although breathtakingly beautiful to human eyes, their green coloration allows the serpents to disappear amid the green foliage of the rainforest canopy. Their sedentary, nocturnal lifestyle means that these snakes move relatively little while in the canopy, thus reducing the chances that predators will see them.

At night, when the darkness covers their movements, the snakes travel down to the lower branches and vines, often within striking distance of the ground. They adopt ambush postures and wait – sometimes for six hours or more – for unsuspecting prey to walk beneath them. They may do this for days or weeks before successfully capturing a meal, but because they exhibit a relatively low energy lifestyle, they manage to thrive.

To a witness living in the New Guinea rainforest, it must surely appear as though the rainforest simply came alive, strangled some rodent or lizard, and consumed it whole.

***

Juvenile green tree pythons are not green at all. They are usually some form of red or yellow, although occasional specimens defy simple descriptions. They become green around 1 or 2 years of age.

This difference in color between adults and juveniles is one of the most striking examples found in any snake species. As one would expect, this incredible trait is adaptive, and it provides a significant benefit for the species as a whole.

While green tree pythons are remarkably camouflaged in the canopy and large enough to eat the rodents and birds running through the dark forest interior, the brightly colored juveniles are conspicuous in this habitat, and they are unable to catch enough suitable food.

Young green tree pythons are very small snakes, and they are not large enough to eat rodents in the wild (and unlike in captivity, where keepers often feed newborn mice to baby green tree pythons, wild newborn rodents stay in burrows). Instead, they rely on ectothermic prey, such as lizards, insects and frogs.

These types of animals are often most abundant in forest edges, such as those made by tree falls or along rivers. In these places, more sunlight reaches the ground. This causes these areas to support a different collection of flora and fauna than those found under the closed canopy. Unlike the forest interior, young green tree pythons find ample food in these habitats.

However, because the flora and structure of these areas are different from those of the closed forest, green is not as effective a color for the young snakes. Instead, colors like yellow and red provide effective camouflage.

***

By most measures, green tree pythons are among the most desirable snakes in the world. Affectionately called "chondros" in reference to their former scientific name, these pretty snakes always draw a crowd at reptile expos and pet stores.

Aside from their incredible beauty, green tree pythons are the perfect size for a pet snake. They are relatively sedentary, so they do not require large cages, and with careful cage design, they will usually perch front-and-center, which allows for excellent viewing opportunities. This makes them much more interesting captives than many of their python cousins, who spend most of their time hiding.

Once established and healthy, green tree python husbandry is rather straightforward. Nevertheless, they still offer plenty of surprises for even the most experienced keepers. Advanced keepers continually debate the merits of various strategies and tactics, and questions outnumber answers.

It took a long time to develop a standard husbandry protocol for these snakes. For years, these beautiful serpents were rarely available for purchase. Those that did surface were invariably stressed, dehydrated and parasitized snakes. Even the world's best keepers struggled to maintain these snakes; breeding green tree pythons was a pipe dream.

Fortunately for snake enthusiasts, keepers kept working with the snakes, and eventually, they began maintaining them successfully. Eventually, captive reproduction occurred.

Now, many years later, green tree pythons are widely available. While imported individuals still appear in the marketplace, many captive bred offspring are available each year. Captive bred offspring are better suited for captivity than their wild caught counterparts are, and they are more likely to thrive in their keeper's hands.

Green tree pythons are not ideal first snakes. However, those, who have already maintained a pet corn snake or ball python, are likely ready to try keeping one of these amazing snakes.

Chapter 1: Green Tree Python Basics

1) Description and Anatomy

Size

Green tree pythons are rather small by python standards. Adult green tree pythons are usually about 5-feet (1.5 meters) long. The longest animals on record slightly exceed 7 feet in length (2.2 meters) (Hillman).

Hatchlings vary in size, but most are approximately 12 inches long and weigh about 10 to 12 grams.

Scalation

Green tree pythons have smooth scales. Green tree pythons have between 50 and 75 scale rows at midbody. They have 225 to 260 ventral scales and 90 to 110 subcaudal scales. Most of the subcaudals are divided.

The heads of green tree pythons are quite beautiful. They are completely covered in numerous irregular, granular scales, except for a few moderately enlarged scales near the nostrils and directly above the mouth (supralabials).

Green tree pythons are very thin-skinned snakes.

Hatchling Color and Pattern

Green tree pythons are not green when they emerge from their eggs. Instead, the young are essentially red or yellow, although there is great variation within these two forms.

Red hatchlings can be virtually any shade of red, from bright "tomato" red to brownish, "brick" red. Some of the yellow babies are very pale, while others are very rich, "lemon" yellow.

Both red and yellow babies also possess small markings along their vertebral line and sides. Many of these take the form of small triangles, or "saw tooth" markings, while others are simply dashes, dots or blotches. Sometimes the lines along the back are connected and they form a continuous stripe, but the line is frequently broken at some point.

A beautiful red-phase hatchling. Note the bright yellow markings along the back.

The markings on red babies often have black outlines. The interior of hollow markings may be red, but they may also feature yellow or white scales. Yellow babies usually have brown-outlined markings that may or may not have white scales inside hollow portions of the markings.

The tails of hatchlings are covered in small patches of black, white and red or yellow scales.

The relative prevalence of the two different color phases differs from one geographic area to the next. In general, yellow hatchlings are more common than red hatchlings, but this is not true in all areas.

Hatchling green tree pythons from the southern portion of their range are typically yellow. This includes those from Australia and those hailing from the south side of the central Papuan mountain range.

By contrast, red is more common among snakes from the Biak island group and some of the highland areas.

Some keepers have hypothesized that the red hatchling color is dominant to the yellow hatchling color. While this pattern generally holds true, several exceptions have occurred. Currently, the pattern of inheritance for the color variations remains unclear.

Ontogenetic Color Shift

Green tree pythons undergo a spectacular ontogenetic (age related) shift in color and pattern. Over time, the bright yellow and red young become green. The shift in color appears to relate to a similar, ontogenetic shift in habitat and foraging strategy.

The onset and duration of the ontogenetic color shift varies widely among individuals, geographic races and selectively bred bloodlines.

Some individuals change colors while relatively small, whereas others are nearly mature before they undergo color change. Some individuals may change colors in a matter of hours, while others take years to complete the color change.

The actual color change can occur in a variety of ways. While there is great variation among individuals from different geographic areas and between different captive lineages, many color changes occur in one of a few archetypal manners:

- The simplest type of color change occurs in many yellow hatchlings from the southern portions of Papua and Australia. These snakes often transform from bright yellow to bright green over the course of a few days. In such circumstances, the yellow scales gradually appear to change to a dirty yellow-green color, before gradually darkening to green. Snakes in the middle of such color changes are certainly interesting and unusual looking, but they are not what most keepers would consider attractive. Fortunately, these types of color changes are usually quick.

- Others remain largely yellow animals, but individual scales begin turning deep green. Over time, more and more yellow scales become completely green. Some of the brown markings begin changing to blue at this time. White scales may appear, disappear or remain unchanged during this time. This form of color change is often quite beautiful and can produce striking blue, yellow and green animals.
- Red animals change colors in a variety of ways. Some become very dark, occasionally gaining black scales during their transition to green. Others lighten, becoming nearly yellow before transitioning to green. Some animals remain orange for an extended period of time -- particularly red animals of Biak ancestry.

On average, green tree pythons change color at about the same time that their diet shifts from primarily ectothermic animals to primarily endothermic animals. This corresponds with a length of about 24 inches (60 centimeters) (Hillman).

According to a 2006 study by D. Wilson, R. Heinsohn and J. Wood that examined the life history and process of color change in a population of Australian green tree pythons found that the snakes all changed color at about the same time. All of the snakes examined in the study below 22 inches in snout-to-vent length were yellow, and all of the snakes over 23 ½ inches in length were green (D. Wilson, 2006).

The study's authors assert that this color change occurred between roughly 11 and 13 months of age. The duration of the change was about eight days (D. Wilson, 2006).

In contrast to Australian specimens, animals originating from Biak are famous for their prolonged color change, which often occurs over a period of several years. In fact, many continue to gain green as mature adults.

Adult Color and Pattern

Adult green tree pythons are essentially green snakes with various blue, white or yellow markings. Nevertheless, there is great variation within this general appearance.

The green color of the pythons varies from mustard- or yellow-green to bright, lime green to deep, emerald green. Some green tree pythons have a considerable amount of blue to their coloration, producing snakes from aqua to powder blue.

A very few albino green tree pythons exist in captivity. In these snakes, the green is replaced with yellow-orange. The adults of a few island populations, notably the Kofiau islands, remain yellow into adulthood. However, completely yellow snakes have turned completely green in a matter of hours or days in some circumstances. The mechanism behind this color change is not well understood.

Many of the markings of green tree pythons tend to be more common among some regional populations and captive lineages. For example, many of the snakes from the northern and central portion of New Guinea have continuous, blue dorsal stripes. The blue stripe may feature lateral extensions that take the form of teardrops, triangles or blotches. Some specific areas, for instance, Manokwari, frequently feature a broken dorsal stripe.

Snakes from Aru seldom exhibit stripes, but they often feature a significant amount of blue dots and flecks. Aru specimens also tend to feature blue markings along their white ventral surfaces.

Many green tree pythons have scattered white scales. They are usually located on the dorsal and lateral surfaces of the snake.

Black flecks tend to occur on highland specimens. Many Biak animals also feature black spots.

Adult green tree pythons may have green, black, blue, white or yellow tails.

Skeletal System

Snakes have elongated bodies, so they have many more vertebrae than most other vertebrates do. Each vertebrae attaches to two of the python's rib bones. The degree of flexibility between each vertebra is much greater in constricting snakes, such as green tree pythons, than it is in most non-constricting snakes.

As demonstrated by their skeletal systems, green tree pythons are very primitive snakes. Unlike advanced snakes that hail from more recent lineages, green tree pythons have retained the pelvic girdle of their lizard ancestors. However, like all living snakes, green tree pythons show no trace of shoulder girdles.

Extending from the pelvic girdle are two rudimentary leg bones. Horny caps cover the end of these bones and penetrate through the body wall, extending outside of the snake's body. Snake keepers often refer to these appendages as "spurs."

Green tree pythons have control over their spurs, but they do not use them for locomotion. Males use their spurs to stimulate females during courting. Very large males often have considerably massive spurs, which can cause serious scratches when handled carelessly.

The difference in size between the spurs of males and females is variable. Accordingly, spur size is not suitable as a method for determining gender. In addition to individual variability, spurs can break and wear down.

Internal Organs

Snakes have internal organs that largely mirror those of other vertebrates, with a few exceptions.

The digestive system of snakes is relatively similar to those of vertebrates, featuring an esophagus that accepts food from the mouth and transports it to the stomach, followed by long intestines that transport food from the stomach to the anus where the food residue is expelled. Along the way, the liver, gall bladder, spleen and pancreas aid the digestive process by producing and storing digestive enzymes.

Snakes propel blood through their bodies via a heart and circulatory system. Unlike advanced snakes (such as rat snakes, kingsnakes, vipers and elapids), green tree pythons are very primitive snakes that retain a full-sized – but nonfunctioning – left lung.

Like those of many other arboreal snakes, the hearts of green tree pythons reside in a relatively anterior position relative to terrestrial serpents. This is thought to be an adaptation that prevents blood-flow problems for the snakes' brains, while they are climbing or resting in unusual postures. (Harvey B. Lillywhitea, 2012)

Like most other animals, snakes have two kidneys, but the kidneys are positioned in a staggered alignment. This allows them to fit inside the body cavity. Snakes produce uric acid as a byproduct of protein synthesis, and expel it through the vent. This uric acid often looks like pieces of chalk, and is not soluble in water.

The nervous system of snakes is largely similar to that of other animals. The brain – which is relatively small and primitive – provides the control over the body by sending impulses through the spinal cord and nerves.

One interesting anatomical feature of green tree pythons (and snakes in general) is their flexible windpipe. Known as the glottis, the tube transports air to and from the lungs and resides in the bottom of snakes' mouths. Snakes have the ability to move their glottis in order to breathe while they are swallowing large food items.

Reproductive Organs
Males have paired reproductive structures that they hold inside their tail base. The males evert these organs, termed hemipenes (singular: hemipenis), during mating activities and insert them inside the females' cloacas.

Females have paired reproductive systems, which essentially mirror those of other vertebrates. One key difference is the presence of structures called oviducts. Oviducts hold the male's sperm and accept the ova after they are released from the ovaries during ovulation.

Head

Unlike the helmet-like skull of mammals, the skull of snakes is a loosely articulated collection of strut- and plate-like bones. This allows them to open their mouth wide enough to eat large prey.

Contrary to popular perception, snakes do not dislocate their jaws when swallowing prey. They simply possess more complex joints than most other animals do. Instead of the mandible connecting directly to the skull (as occurs in humans and most other vertebrates), the mandible of snakes connects to the quadrate bone. The quadrate bone, in turn, connects to the skull. This arrangement allows the quadrate bone to swing down and forward, while the mandible pivots downward and forward as well.

The jaw's loose articulation also allows it to widen slightly, once open. The lower mandible is split at the chin, allowing the two bones to spread apart.

Eyes and Ears

Most green tree pythons see movement well, but their visual acuity may be limited. Green tree pythons see well during both the day and the night. While not the most important sensory pathway for green tree pythons, (many have survived injuries that left them blind) their sense of sight provides them with a number of advantages.

Snakes lack moveable eyelids, meaning that their eyes are open at all times – even while they sleep. In fact, it can be difficult (or impossible) to tell whether a motionless snake is sleeping or awake. To protect their eyes, snakes have a clear scale covering each eye, called spectacles. Like all other scales on the snake's body, they shed their spectacles periodically.

Green tree pythons have elliptical pupils that resemble those of a cat. While frequently presumed to be a trait associated with nocturnal activity patterns, recent research indicates that such eyes are more likely an adaptation to ambush – rather than prowling – hunting styles (F. BRISCHOUX, 2010).

Snakes lack external ears, but they do have rudimentary middle and inner ears. Part of the reason for this is that the bones which normal reside in the ears of mammals have moved to the jaws of snakes. They now serve as the quadrate bone! Accordingly, snakes hear very few, if any, sounds. Scientists debate the finer points of their abilities, but snakes do not appear to respond to most airborne sounds. However, snakes can feel very low frequency vibrations through the substrate, such as footsteps.

Thermally Receptive Pits
The upper lip scales of green tree pythons have small indentations. Nerves connecting to the bottom of these depressions carry thermal information to the brain. In the brain, this thermal information is superimposed over visual information. The result is that green tree pythons (and similarly equipped pythons and pit vipers) are able to "see" heat.

This helps the snakes in myriad ways. The difference in temperature between a warm-blooded bird or rodent and the cool night air makes such prey conspicuous, regardless of their cryptic efforts or morphology. Similarly, the snakes can better see warm-blooded predators at a distance, and act accordingly.

The thermo-receptive pits are visible in this photograph. Note the rectangular depressions below the mouth.

It is also likely that green tree pythons and similarly equipped snakes use the information derived from the pits to aid their thermoregulatory behavior. It may also play a role in egg incubation.

Tongue, Nose and Vomeronasal Organ
The forked tongue of snakes is one of their most famous characteristics. It is exclusively a sensory organ, and it plays no role in feeding or sound production.

The tongue extends from the mouth to collect volatile particles from the environment. Then, when the tongue is withdrawn, it transfers these particles to the vomeronasal organ. The vomeronasal organ provides the snakes with an additional chemical sense, like smell and taste.

The vomeronasal organ (located in the roof of the mouth), has two openings – one for each tip of the snake's tongue. This allows snakes to process directional information picked up by the tongue. Snakes also use their nostrils to detect airborne chemicals in the environment, and have a very strong sense of smell.

Mouth and Teeth
Green tree pythons have approximately 100 sharp, pointed teeth, designed for catching and holding prey. As with all other pythons, green tree pythons have five pairs of bones that hold their teeth. These are known as the premaxillary, maxillary, palantine, pterygoid and dentary bones.

The premaxillary bones hold the teeth directly under the pythons' nostrils. Green tree pythons typically have one small tooth on each premaxillary bone. The premaxillaries each abut a maxillary. The maxillaries hold about 17 teeth on each side.

Pythons also bear teeth on the roof of their mouths in two parallel rows. Each row is comprised of teeth borne on two different bones – the palantine bone is located at the anterior portion of the mouth and the pterygoid bone is located at the rear of the mouth. Combined, the two bones create a row of 16 teeth on each side of the mouth.

The teeth of the bottom jaw attach to the dentary bones. Each dentary holds about 16 teeth (Barker, 1994).

When looking at the mouth of a living green tree python, you will find that the bottom and top jaws both have a row of teeth along the periphery of the mouth (the premaxillary, maxillary and dentary bones), while the palate has two parallel rows of teeth (the palantine and pterygoid bones).

The outer row of teeth in the top of the mouth number 36, the number of teeth along the perimeter of the bottom of the mouth total 32, and 2 rows of 16 teeth lie in the roof of the mouth.

The four to eight anterior-most teeth of the maxillary and dentary bones are very long and slightly recurved.

Like all snakes, chondros continually lose and replace teeth throughout their lives. Sometimes keepers will find shed teeth in their snake's cage or emerging from feces.

Vent
The vent is the place from which snakes defecate and release urates. Additionally, it is the exit point for their reproductive organs and eggs or young. Inside the vent lies a chamber called the cloaca, which holds these products until they are expelled through the vent.

Tail
While they look like heads that seamlessly transition into tails, the tails of snakes are shorter than many people realize they are. The tail starts at the vent (where the spurs are visible) and travels to the end of the body.

Green tree pythons have extremely prehensile tails, which they use to help grip tree branches (and the arms of their keepers). The tails of green tree pythons are long and very thin; those of hatchlings are unimaginably delicate.

2) Biology

As with their unique anatomy, snakes exhibit unique biology. In many cases, the physiological differences exhibited by snakes are not as fantastic as they seem, once they are viewed in the correct context.

Shedding

Like other animals, snakes must shed their outer skin layers, as they require replacement. While mammals do so continuously, snakes shed their entire external layer of skin cells at periodic intervals.

This process may occur as frequently as once every month when snakes are young and growing quickly, or as rarely as two or three times per year for larger, mature snakes.

Snakes that are injured, ill or parasitized may shed more frequently than usual. Some shedding events, such as the snake's first shed, or the females' post-ovulation shed, mark important milestones.

The shedding process takes approximately 7 to 10 days to complete. Initially, the snake begins producing a layer of fluid between the two outermost layers of skin. This serves as a lubricant that helps the old skin to peel off.

After a day or two, this fluid may become visible and give the snakes a cloudy appearance. It is often most apparent when viewing the snake's ventral surface or eyes. Because clear scales cover the eyes of snakes, the fluid makes the eyes of most pre-shed snakes look very cloudy and blue. At this time, the snake's vision is impaired, and most snakes spend this time hiding. However, relative to other species, the color change associated with shedding is very subtle for green tree pythons Many keepers are surprised when their green tree python sheds.

A few days later, the snake's eyes clear up, and it looks normal again. A day or two later, the snake will begin the process of shedding.

Snakes begin the process starts by trying to cut the old layer of skin on their lips. They do this by rubbing their faces against stationary surfaces. While many keepers incorporate a rough surface in the cage for fear that the snake will not be able to facilitate his shedding process, in practice, this is rarely a problem. The cage walls are usually more than adequate for the purpose.

After separating the skin on the lips, the old skin starts to peel away. The snake crawls forward, leaving the old skin behind. The new skin usually looks much brighter than normal.

Metabolism and Digestion
Snakes are ectothermic ("cold-blooded") animals that rely on external sources of heat to drive their metabolisms. This means that, in general, the warmer a snake is, the faster all of the chemical reactions taking place in its body proceed. Snakes that are not warm enough are not able to move, breathe, think or feel stimuli as well as they should.

Fortunately for green tree pythons, the ambient temperatures in their native lands are close to their ideal body temperature. The few wild studies of the species that have been undertaken have failed to observe green tree pythons engaging in thermoregulatory behavior. However, while gravid, digesting food or recovering from illness, green tree pythons may bask in the sun.

Growth Rate and Lifespan
Green tree pythons studied in the wild generally matured between 2 ½ and 3 ½ years (males and females, respectively), which is consistent with the growth rate of captive green tree pythons. (D. Wilson, 2006)

Males are mature at snout-to-vent lengths of approximately 33 inches (84 centimeters), while females reach maturity at about 39 inches (99 centimeters).

According to the growth rate of green tree pythons D. Wilson, et al, calculated the maximum life expectancy of green tree pythons as 19 years. However, a few captive snakes have exceeded this figure.

Green tree pythons grow relatively little after reaching sexual maturity. Females grow to slightly larger sizes than males do, but the differences in size are relatively minor.

3) Behavior

While green tree pythons are among the most sedentary snakes in the world, they do exhibit a number of interesting behaviors.

Hunting and Constriction

While there is some evidence that suggests green tree pythons occasionally prowl for food, they are primarily ambush hunters. Green tree pythons wrap several coils of their bodies around a perch and extend the front half of their body in an "S" shape.

When prey approaches, they will quickly strike the animal, secure it with their jaws and pull it towards them while wrapping coils around the prey's body. This all happens incredibly quickly, and appears to be one fluid motion.

The python will squeeze the prey animal until it stops breathing, at which time they will release the pressure and begin searching for the prey's head. Like all snakes, green tree pythons swallow their prey whole.

Many green tree pythons – particularly juveniles – exhibit a behavior known as "caudal luring." To do so, green tree pythons adopt an ambush hunting posture and then lower their (often conspicuously colored) tail tips below them. They then begin to twitch and wiggle their tails in a manner reminiscent of a worm or caterpillar.

When a lizard or other creature sees the "worm," it approaches the perceived meal. However, as the prey approaches, the snake strikes out and captures the would-be-hunter.

Diel Activity

Green tree pythons may be active at any hour of the day. Adults are primarily nocturnal animals, while hatchlings tend to be diurnal.

A 2006 study of Australian green tree pythons found that the snakes were typically active between 6:00pm and 8:00pm, as they moved from their daytime perches to their nighttime hunting perches. The snakes did not change ambush locations during the night, instead remaining loyal to a single perch for the duration of the night. Between 4:00am and 8:00am, the snakes would return to their daytime perches (Wilson, 2006).

By contrast, juveniles in the study exhibited diurnal activity patterns. The young yellow snakes (no red snakes were present in the study) would attempt to ambush small lizards and invertebrates during the day.

Both the juveniles and adults tended to move closer to the ground while hunting (D. Wilson, 2006).

Seasonal Activity

The seasonal activity of green tree pythons is poorly understood. All green tree pythons live in areas with consistently warm temperatures, allowing them to be active all year.

The rainfall, however, varies significantly in many of the locations in which green tree pythons live. Most areas have a distinct wet season, and a slightly drier season. However, the timing of the rainy season varies from one area to the next.

Note, for example, the different rainy seasons in the following locations:

Region	Rainy Season
Wamena	September to February
Aru Islands	November to March
Merauke	December to April
Jayapura	December to April
Port Moresby	December to April
Manokwari	December to May
Cape York Peninsula	January to March
Biak Island	January to June

Green tree pythons exhibit a seasonal reproductive schedule in Australia, but most specimens from New Guinea have not been studied.

In Australia, the adults breed in the wet season, and hatchlings emerge from their eggs in November. Nevertheless, captive green tree pythons have produced eggs in virtually every month of the year.

Defensive Strategies and Tactics

Green tree pythons primarily rely on their crypsis, sedentary habits and diel activity patterns for protection. The green coloration of the adults provides very effective camouflage with the leafy, green canopy, while the yellow and red babies camouflage well in brightly lit situations and the forest understory, respectively.

If their cryptic coloration fails them, green tree pythons often hide their head within their coils as an initial defense. If the attacker persists, green tree pythons may hiss and twitch violently, in efforts to thwart the unwanted attention.

If these efforts fail, chondros may attempt to bite their perceived attacker. Despite their small size and lack of venom, green tree python dentition is impressive, and the pythons can deliver a serious bite.

In all circumstances, green tree pythons are very reluctant to release their grip on their perch – even after continuous attacks that may cause other species to attempt to flee.

Interestingly, most snakes grip their perches much tighter than necessary. Some species have been known to exert three times the pressure necessary to keep the snake from falling. This may be a response to the height at which these snakes climb, and the danger of falling.

Green tree pythons may discharge musk or defecate on perceived aggressors, but it is not a common behavior.

Locomotion
While they may employ several different methods of locomotion, green tree pythons primarily crawl via a method called rectilinear motion and climb via a method called concertina motion. Green tree pythons do not hold a monopoly on the method -- rectilinear motion is the most common method of crawling for many large-bodied snakes, including pythons and vipers.

Rectilinear motion occurs when the green tree pythons use a section of their ventral and lateral muscles to swing their ventral scales forward, grip the substrate, and then pull the snake forward. The process allows the snakes to crawl forward smoothly, in a straight line.

Concertina motion involves extending the head and neck in the direction of an accessible perch. The head and chin then grip and pull against the perch, which brings the python's rear body forward.

Like most snakes, green tree pythons are capable swimmers, though it must surely be a rare occurrence for wild specimens. Nevertheless, green tree pythons do not appear to enjoy swimming, and they usually look for the first opportunity to exit the water.

4) Reproduction

Very little information exists regarding the wild breeding habits of green tree pythons. Most of the information that does exist regarding breeding biology and behavior comes from captive breeders in the United States and Europe, as well as green tree python "farmers" in Southeast Asia.

Like all pythons, female green tree pythons coil around their clutch after depositing eggs. They do so to protect the eggs from predators, guard against desiccation and ensure that the eggs remain warm enough to develop properly.

The females accomplish the last goal through a series of muscular "twitches" or "shivers." These small movements warm the body of the female, which in turn warms the eggs.

The young hatch approximately 50 to 55 days later, and the mother leaves soon thereafter. To escape from the eggs, the young snakes use a small sharp egg tooth, which will fall off shortly after hatching.

Chapter 2: Classification and Taxonomy

Green tree pythons are one of the 40-odd species of python currently recognized. In the past, scientists placed green tree pythons on a few different branches of the python family tree. However, most authorities agree that they are correctly placed within the genus Morelia, as it is currently construed.

Scientists formerly classified these snakes as the sole members of the genus *Chondropython*. This classification scheme was based on the mistaken notion that green tree pythons lacked teeth on their premaxillary bones. Since this correction, they have remained in the genus *Morelia*.

Green tree pythons clearly have some similarities with carpet pythons, and hybrids of the two species have been produced in captivity. However, most researchers consider rough scaled pythons to be the closest living relatives of green tree pythons.

Green tree pythons are currently classified as follows:

Kingdom: Animalia

Phylum: Chordata

Class: Reptilia

Order: Squamata

Family: Boidae / Pythonidae

Genus: Morelia

Species: viridis

In 2002, L. H. Rawlings and Stephen C. Donnellan completed a study of green tree pythons and found some interesting patterns. According to the study – which investigated the mitochondrial DNA and alloenzymes of the species – green tree pythons occur in two distinct forms: a northern and southern form.

The primary dividing line between northern and southern populations is the mountain range that travels across the center of New Guinea.

The two are not yet recognized as subspecies or different species, but this may change in the future. The two different forms have successfully produced offspring together numerous times in captivity (Donnellan, 2003).

Minor morphological differences characterize both the northern and southern form, but they freely interbreed in captivity.

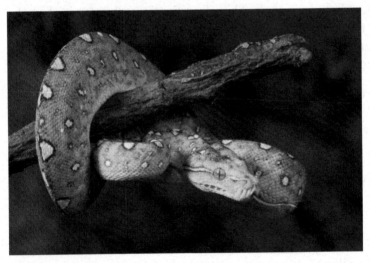

This Biak-type hatchling was originally a red baby. However, as it progressed through its color change, it became light orange before transitioning to green.

Chapter 3: The Green Tree Python's World

Understanding the world of green tree pythons is best accomplished by considering their geographic range, habitat preferences and ecology.

1) Range

Green tree pythons are found throughout the island of New Guinea, several of its offshore islands and the northern portions of the Cape York Peninsula in Australia. They have been reported from sea level to 6,500 feet (2,000 meters) in elevation, but many are skeptical that the snakes live this high in the mountains.

2) Habitat

Green tree pythons typically inhabit primary, evergreen, broadleaf rainforests. Juveniles who have not yet changed color inhabit clearings and edges, while the adults inhabit closed-canopy areas. Green tree pythons inhabit a broad vertical range, extending from ground level to the middle of the canopy.

3) Natural Diet

Green tree pythons are opportunistic, generalist carnivores that primarily consume lizards and invertebrates while young, and rodents, lizards and birds when mature.

The relative abundance of birds in the diet of green tree pythons has been a contested issue. Early writers, impressed with the snakes' dentition, often speculated that the teeth were adapted for getting through the feathers of birds. However, as more data was collected, it became apparent that birds, while occasionally taken, represented a small portion of the species' diet. In actuality, the long front teeth of green tree pythons are likely an adaptation that helps them to grip their prey securely, while the pythons are suspended upside down. Documented prey of green tree pythons includes:

- Cape York Mosaic-Tailed Rat (*Melomys capensis*)
- House Mouse (*Mus domesticus*)
- Closed-Litter Rainbow Skink (*Carlia longipes*)
- Paradise Riflebird (*Ptiloris paradiseus*)

(Wilson D. , 2007)

Additionally, various rats, skinks, geckos, beetles, moths and other mammals have been documented, but their exact identification were either not recorded or not known.

4) Natural Predators

The most significant predators for chondros are likely predatory birds. Additionally, large monitor lizards (*Varanus* sp.) dingoes and medium-sized mammalian predators, such as quolls (*Dasyurus* sp.) consume green tree pythons from time to time.

Humans living in New Guinea also eat green tree pythons, but they are not thought to be a significant source of mortality for the snakes. Two indirect forms of human-caused mortality – automobile collisions and collection for the pet trade – are more impactful than human predation is on wild populations.

Birds that likely predate on green tree pythons include:

- Grey Goshawks (*Accipiter novaehollandiae*)
- Long-tailed Buzzards (*Accipiter longicauda*)
- Meyer's Goshawk (*Accipiter meyerianus*)
- Grey-headed Goshawk (*Accipiter poliocephalus*)
- Black-Mantled Goshawk (*Accipiter melanochlamys*)
- Chestnut-Shouldered Goshawk (*Accipiter buergersi*)
- Doria's Hawk (*Megatriorchis doriae*)
- Rufous Owl (*Ninox rufa*)

- Harpy Eagle (*Harpiopsis novaeguineae*)
- Black Butcherbird (*Cracticus quoyi*)

(David Wilson, 2007)

Chapter 4: The Green Tree Python as a Pet

While green tree pythons can make great pets, there are a number of things to consider before you acquire one of your own. Green tree pythons are living, breathing creatures that deserve the highest quality of life possible.

1) Understanding the Commitment

You will be responsible for your snake's well-being for the rest of its life. This is important to understand, as green tree pythons may live to be 20 years of age or more. Can you be sure that you will still want to care for your pet in 15 or 20 years?

It is not your snake's fault if your interests change. Neglecting your snake is wrong, and in some locations, a criminal offense. You must never neglect your pet, even once the novelty has worn off, and it is no longer fun to clean the cage.

Once you purchase a green tree python, its well-being becomes your responsibility until it passes away at the end of a long life, or you have found someone who will agree to take over the care of the animal for you. Understand that it may be very difficult to find someone who will adopt it for you.

Never release a pet snake into the wild.

Snakes introduced to places outside their native range can cause a variety of harmful effects on the ecosystem. Even if the snake is native to the region, it is possible that it has been infected with pathogens. If released into the wild, these pathogens may run rampant through the local population, causing horrific die offs. In the case of green tree pythons, they are sure to perish if released in any habitat other than their native rainforests.

2) The Costs of Captivity

Keeping a snake is much less expensive than many other pets; however, novices frequently fail to consider the total costs of purchasing the snake, its habitat, food and other supplies. In addition to the up-front costs, there are on-going costs as well.

Startup Costs

One surprising fact for most new keepers is that the enclosure and equipment may cost more than the animal does (this is not always the case with high-priced snakes). This may not be true when purchasing your first green tree python, as juveniles can be kept in very simple enclosures.

Prices fluctuate from one market to the next, but in general, the least you will spend on the snake is about $300 (£185). The least you will spend on the *initial* habitat and assorted equipment will be about $50 (£29). Conversely, you do not have to look too hard to find green tree pythons with five-figure price tags – green tree python connoisseurs seldom lack ways to spend money on their hobby.

Breeders and those with large collections often implement systems that reduce the per-snake housing costs, sometimes getting the costs down to one quarter of that price. However, for the hobbyist with a pet snake or two, such options are not helpful or appropriate.

Examine the charts on the following pages to get an idea of three different pricing scenarios. While the specific prices listed will vary based on numerous variables, the charts are instructive for first-time buyers. The first scenario details a keeper who is trying to spend as little as possible, while the second provides a middle-of-the-road example. The third example is of a more extravagant shopper, who wants an expensive snake, and top-notch equipment. These charts do not cover all of the costs necessary at startup, such as the initial veterinary visit, shipping charges for the snake or any of the equipment (which can easily exceed $100) or the initial food purchase. These charts also fail to allocate anything decorative items, and they assume the use of newspaper as a substrate, which is essentially free.

Inexpensive Option

Entry-Level Green Tree Python	$300 (£185)
Plastic Storage Box	$10 (£6)
Screen and Hardware for Lid	$10 (£6)
Heat Lamp Fixture and Bulbs	$20 (£11)
Digital Indoor-Outdoor Thermometer	$15 (£9)
Infrared Thermometer	$35 (£20)
Water Dish	$5 (£3)
Forceps, Spray Bottles, Misc. Supplies	$20 (£11)
Total	**$415 (£256)**

Moderate Option

Mid-Range Green Tree Python	$500 (£310)
20-Gallon Aquarium	$40 (£24)
Screen Lid	$10 (£6)
Heat Lamp Fixture and Bulbs	$20 (£11)
Digital Indoor-Outdoor Thermometer	$15 (£6)
Infrared Thermometer	$35 (£20)
Water Dish	$5 (£3)
Forceps, Spray Bottles, Misc. Supplies	$20 (£11)
Total	**$645 (£400)**

Premium Option

Premium Green Tree Python	$2000 (£209)
Commercial Plastic Cage	$150 (£87)
Radiant Heat Panel	$75 (£44)
Thermostat	$50 (£29)
Digital Indoor-Outdoor Thermometer	$15 (£6)
Infrared Thermometer	$35 (£20)
Water Dish	$5 (£3)
Forceps, Spray Bottles, Misc. Supplies	$20 (£11)
Total	**$2350 (£1450)**

Ongoing Costs

Once you have your snake and his habitat, you must still be able to afford regular care and maintenance. While snakes are low-cost pets, this must be viewed in context.

Compared to a 100-pound Labrador retriever, a snake is relatively inexpensive. However, when compared to a goldfish, tarantula or hermit crab, snakes are fantastically expensive.

Here is an example of the ongoing costs a typical snake keeper must endure. Remember: Emergencies can and will happen. You must have some way to weather these storms, and afford a sudden veterinary bill, or the cost to replace a cage that breaks unexpectedly.

The three primary ongoing costs for snake are:

- **Veterinary Costs**
  While experienced keepers may be able to avoid going to the vet for regular examinations, novices should visit their veterinarian at least once every year. Assuming your snake is healthy, you may only need to pay for an office visit. However, if your vet sees signs of illness, you may find yourself paying for cultures, medications or procedures. Wise keepers budget at least $200 to $300 (£117 to £175) for veterinary costs each year.

- **Food Costs**
  Food is the single greatest ongoing cost you will experience while caring for your green tree python. To obtain a reasonable estimate of your yearly food costs, you must consider the number of meals you will feed your snake per year and the cost of each meal.

Most green tree pythons will consume between 25 and 50 food items per year. In general, younger snakes should be fed about once per week, while adults may be fed about half as often (although some keepers continue to feed their adults weekly – see FEEDING chapter for further discussion).

Hatchling green tree pythons will eat "fuzzy" or "hopper" mice; large adults require large mice or small rats. So you will need between 50 fuzzy mice and 25 small rats.

The cost of feeder rodents varies drastically depending upon the source. It is much cheaper to purchase them in bulk, but you must have the freezer space to store the feeders. However, you may need to allow for shipping costs when purchasing bulk rodents. Retail rodents typically cost about three times the price of those purchased in bulk.

For example, fuzzy mice may cost $0.25 or so each, when purchased in bulk. A single fuzzy mouse in a pet store is likely to cost $1.00 or more. Likewise, a small rat is about $1.00 when purchased in bulk, but will cost you at least $3.00 to purchase from a pet store.

Extrapolated over the course of a year, these differences become significant. For example, if may cost you about $13 to purchase 50 fuzzy mice in bulk, or $50 to purchase them from your local pet shop. As long as the shipping costs are less than $37, it makes more sense to purchase the animals in bulk.

- **Maintenance Costs**
  It is important to plan for routine and unexpected maintenance costs. Commonly used items, such as paper towels, disinfectant and cypress mulch are rather easy to calculate. However, it is not easy to know how many burned out light bulbs, cracked water dishes or faulty thermostats you will have to replace in a given year.

  Those who keep small green tree pythons in simple enclosures will likely find that $50 (£29) covers their yearly maintenance costs. By contrast, those keeping large green tree pythons in elaborate habitats may spend $200 (£117) or more each year.

Always try to purchase frequently used supplies, such as light bulbs, paper towels and disinfectants in bulk to maximize your savings. It is often beneficial to consult with local reptile-keeping clubs, who often use their members combined needs to make purchases in bulk.

3) Myths and Misunderstandings

Snakes are the subject for countless myths and misunderstandings. It is important to rectify any flawed perceptions before welcoming a snake into your life.

Myth: Snakes grow in proportion to the size of their cage and then stop.

Fact: Snakes do no such thing. Healthy snakes grow throughout their lives, although the rate of growth slows with age. Placing them in a small cage in an attempt to stunt their growth is an unthinkably cruel practice, which is more likely to sicken or kill the snake than stunt its growth.

Myth: Snakes can sense fear.

Fact: Snakes are not magical creatures. They are constrained by physics and biology just as humans, dogs and squid are. With that said, it is possible for some animals to read human body language very well. Some long-time keepers have noticed differences in the behavior of some snakes when people of varying comfort levels handle them. This difference in behavior may be confused with the snake "sensing fear."

Myth: Snakes must eat live food.

Fact: While snakes primarily hunt live prey in the wild, some species consume carrion when the opportunity presents itself. In captivity, most snakes learn to accept dead prey. Whenever possible, hobbyists should feed dead prey to their snakes to minimize the suffering of the prey animal and reduce the chances that the snake will become injured.

Myth: Snakes have no emotions and do not suffer.

Fact: While snakes have very primitive brains, and do not have emotions comparable to those of higher mammals, they can absolutely suffer. Always treat snakes with the same compassion you would offer a dog, cat or horse.

Myth: Snakes prefer elaborately decorated cages that resemble their natural habitat.

Fact: While some snakes thrive better in complex habitats that offer a variety of hiding and thermoregulatory options, they do not appreciate your aesthetic efforts.

Unlike humans, who experience the world through their eyes, snakes experience the world largely as they perceive it through their vomeronasal system. Your green tree python is not impressed with the rainforest wallpaper decorating the walls of his cage.

Additionally, while many snakes require hiding spaces, they do not seem to mind whether this hiding space is in the form of a rock, a rotten log or a paper plate. As long as the hiding spot is safe and snug, they will utilize it.

Myth: Green tree pythons automatically constrict any animal with which they come into contact.

Fact: Green tree pythons are very strong constrictors, but they do not engage in constricting behavior unless they are trying to subdue prey or, rarely, when defending themselves from predators. However, when held, green tree pythons often hang on tightly, but this is of little concern. Nevertheless, it is a bad idea to allow any constricting snake to wrap around your neck.

Myth: Chondros are vicious snakes that are quick to bite.

Fact: Green tree pythons have a reputation for being aggressive snakes. Fortunately, for those drawn to these beautiful snakes, this reputation is overstated.

In actuality, green tree pythons exhibit a range of personalities. Some are tame, trusting and docile, while others are defensive and quick to bite when touched. Still others are such aggressive eaters that they appear to be inclined to bite, even though they do not feel threatened by their keeper. The vast majority are somewhat shy, and content to hide their head among their coils when gently manipulated.

Green tree pythons are not "lap snakes," and should be treated accordingly. Some permit gentle handling, while others will vehemently resist your attempts to hold them. In general, it is still easy to manage even the most aggressive green tree pythons by using removable perches.

The reputation probably arose from early keepers, who had no choice but to deal with wild caught animals. As with many other species, wild caught individuals can be defensive, and captive bred individuals are usually calmer.

4) Acquisition and Selection

There are three primary considerations to make when selecting a green tree python: gender, age and personality.

The Gender
Aside from breeding attempts, the husbandry of green tree pythons is essentially identical for both genders. The females do grow slightly larger than males do in the wild, but the difference in size between the two is subtle – female green tree pythons do not require substantially larger cages than males do.

Accordingly, both genders can make suitable pets. Because green tree pythons should not be probed for the first year of their lives, most keepers purchase hatchlings without knowing their genders. Some keepers have asserted that females eat more aggressively than males do, but this has yet to be proven empirically.

If you purchase an older specimen, whose gender is known, it makes slightly more sense to select a male. Because females are in higher demand by breeders, males are often priced lower than females are.

The Age
New keepers should always purchase established animals. Hatchling green tree pythons are often extraordinarily reluctant to initiate feeding, and establishing them requires all of the skill veteran breeders can muster. Fresh hatchlings are completely inappropriate snakes for beginners.

Beginners should always purchase green tree pythons that feed regularly and have shed a few times. Most such snakes will be at least 2 or 3 months old.

When possible, it is even better for beginners to purchase yearlings, who are more forgiving of errors than young animals are.

The Personality
Advanced hobbyists and breeders may consider a snake's personality to be a low priority in comparison to its species, gender, age and other factors. However, for new keepers, personality can be an important criterion. When purchasing year-old or older snakes, beginners can try to select calm individuals (provided they are good feeders). However, when selecting a younger animal, it often behooves the keeper to select an aggressive – but not nervous – animal.

In many cases, aggressive animals are easier to feed.

5) Acquiring Your Green tree python

If, after careful, deliberate, consideration, you choose to purchase a green tree python, you have a number of places from which you can obtain one.

Pet Stores
Pet stores are a common place that many people turn to when they decide to purchase a snake. However, pet stores are not always the best place to purchase a green tree python.

The benefits of shopping at a pet store are that they will likely have all of the equipment you may need, including cages, heating devices and food items. You will usually be able to inspect the snake up close before purchase. In some cases, you may be able to choose from more than one specimen.

Further, many pet stores provide health guarantees for a short period. However, pet stores are retail establishments, and as such, you will pay more than you will from a breeder. Pet stores do not often know the pedigree of the animals they sell, nor are they likely to know the snake's date of birth, or other pertinent information on the snake.

The drawbacks to purchasing a green tree python from a pet store relate to the amount of expertise and knowledge of the staff. While some pet stores concentrate on reptiles and may have a staff capable of providing them with proper care, many green tree pythons languish while living in pet stores.

It is also worth considering the increased exposure to pathogens that pet store animals endure, given the constant flow of animals through the facility.

Reptile Expos
Reptile expos are often excellent places to acquire new animals. Reptile expos often feature resellers, breeders and retailers in the same room, all selling various types of snakes and other reptiles.

Often, the prices at such events are quite reasonable and you are often able to select from many different snakes. However, if you have a problem, it may be difficult to find the seller after the event is over.

Breeders
Breeders are the best place for most novices to shop for green tree pythons. Breeders generally offer unparalleled information and support after the sale. Additionally, breeders often know the species well, and are better able to help you learn the husbandry techniques for the animal.

The disadvantage of buying from a breeder is that you must often make such purchases from a distance, either by phone or via the

Internet. Breeders often have the widest selection of snakes, and are often the only place to find rare forms and truly spectacular specimens.

Classified Advertisements
Newspaper and website classified advertisements sometimes include listings for green tree pythons. While individuals, rather than businesses generally post these, they are a viable option to monitor. Often these sales include a snake and all of the associated equipment, which is convenient for new keepers. However, be careful to avoid purchasing someone else's "problem" (i.e. a snake that does not eat).

6) Quarantine

Because new animals may have illnesses or parasites that could infect the rest of your collection, it is wise to quarantine any new acquisitions. This means that you should keep the new animal as separated from the rest of your pets as much as possible, until you have ensured that the new animal is healthy.

During the quarantine period, you should keep the new snake in a simplified habitat, with a paper substrate, water bowl and perch. Keep the temperature and humidity levels at ideal levels. While the animal is being quarantined, visit the veterinarian to ensure the snake does not have any lurking illnesses. Your veterinarian can also double check to ensure no external parasites are present. If possible, a fecal examination should be conducted, to ensure the animal does not have any internal parasites.

Always tend to quarantined animals last, to reduce the chances of transmitting pathogens to your healthy animals. Do not wash water bowls or cage furniture with those belonging to your healthy animals. Whenever possible, use completely separate tools for quarantined animals and those that have been in your collection for some time.

Always be sure to wash your hands thoroughly after handling quarantined snakes, their cages or their tools. Particularly careful keepers wear a smock or alternative clothing when handling quarantined animals.

Quarantine new acquisitions for a minimum of 30 days; 60 or 90 days is even better. Many zoos and professional breeders maintain 180- or 360-day-long quarantine periods.

Most professional breeders and advanced hobbyists maintain their snakes in a state of perpetual quarantine. While they may be kept in the same room with other chondros, their dishes, hide boxes and cages are not shared.

This beautiful green tree python is beginning to develop blue markings towards the end of the color changing process.

Chapter 5: Providing the Captive Habitat

In most respects, providing green tree pythons with a suitable captive habitat entails functionally replicating the various aspects of their wild habitats. In addition to providing an enclosure, you must provide the right thermal environment, appropriate humidity, substrate, and suitable hiding spots.

1) Enclosure

Providing your green tree python with appropriate housing is and essential aspect of captive care. In essence, the habitat you provide to your snake becomes his "world."

In "the old days," those inclined to keep snakes had few choices with regard to caging. The two primary options were to build a custom cage from scratch or construct a lid to use with a fish aquarium.

By contrast, modern hobbyists have a variety of options from which to choose. In addition to building custom cages or adapting aquaria, dozens of different cage styles are available – each with different pros and cons.

Dimensions
Throughout their lives, snakes need a cage large enough to lay comfortably, access a range of temperatures and get enough room for exercise.

The rule of thumb for most snakes is to ensure that the animal is no longer than ½ the length of the cage's perimeter. However, chonodros are relatively sedentary snakes, and most experienced keepers utilize smaller cages than this.

Hatchlings and young snakes require about 100 to 200 square inches of space. Large, mature animals require about 4 to 6 square feet of space, although some keepers offer slightly more.

Despite their tendency to live high in the canopy, captive green tree pythons do not require very tall cages. Even large adults will thrive in cages with 18 to 24 inches in height – more than this will cause heating and furnishing challenges. Additionally, some snakes may be reluctant to descend to the bottom of the cage to drink from their water bowls.

In addition to total space, the layout of the cage is also important – rectangular cages are strongly preferable for a variety of reasons:

- They allow the keeper to establish better thermal gradients.
- Cages with one long direction allow your snake to stretch out better than a square cage does.
- If the cage is accessible via front-opening doors, you will not have to reach as far back in a rectangular cage when cleaning, as you will a square cage.

Aquariums
Aquariums are popular choices for snake cages, largely because of their ubiquity. Virtually any pet store that carries snakes also stocks aquariums.

Aquariums can make suitable snake cages, but they have a number of drawbacks.

- Aquariums (and other glass cages) are hard to clean
- Aquariums are very fragile
- Aquariums do not retain heat very well
- Aquariums require an after-market or custom built lid
- Aquariums often develop water spots from repeated mistings

When aquariums are used with screened tops, the excess ventilation may cause the tank to dry out rapidly. This can be a challenge for green tree python keepers, who are attempting to keep their cages relatively humid. To work around this, some keepers attach plastic or glass covers over a portion of the screened lid.

Commercial Cages

Commercially produced cages have a number of benefits over other enclosures. Commercial cages usually feature doors on the front of the cage, which provide better access than top-opening cages do. Additionally, bypass glass doors or framed, hinged doors are generally more secure than after-market screened lids are.

Plastic cages are usually produced in dimensions that make more sense for snakes, and often have features that aid in heating and lighting the cage.

Commercial cages can be made out of wood, metal, glass or other substances, but the majority of commercial cages are made from PVC or ABS plastic.

Commercial cages are available in two primary varieties: those that are molded from one piece of plastic and those that are assembled from several different sheets. Assembled cages are less expensive and easier to construct, but molded cages have few (if any) seams or cracks in which bacteria and other pathogens can hide.

Some cage manufacturers produce cages in multiple colors. White is probably the best color for novices, as it is easy to see dirt, mites and other small problems. A single mite crawling on a white cage surface is very visible, even from a distance.

Black cages do not show dirt as well. This can be helpful for more experienced keepers who have developed proper hygiene techniques over time. Additionally, green tree pythons are often beautiful when viewed against black cage walls.

While green tree pythons have cone cells in their retinas, and can presumably see color, it is unlikely that cage color is a significant factor in their quality of life. If you worry about this, it is probably best to choose a dark or earth-toned color.

Plastic Storage Containers

Plastic storage containers, such as those used for shoes, sweaters or food, make suitable cages for small chondros. However, the lids for plastic storage boxes are rarely secure enough for use with snakes.

Hobbyists and breeders overcome this by incorporating Velcro straps, hardware latches or other strategies into plastic storage container cages.

The best way to use plastic storage containers is with a wooden or plastic rack. Such systems are often designed to use containers without lids. In these "lidless" systems, the shelves of the rack form the top to the cage sitting below them. The gap between the top of the sides of the storage containers and the bottom of the shelves is usually very tight – approximately one-eighth inch (2 millimeters) or less.

When plastic containers are used, you must drill or melt numerous holes for air exchange. If you are using a lid, it is acceptable to place the holes in the lid; however, if you are using a lidless system, you will have to make the holes in the sides of the boxes.

Drill or melt all of the holes from the inside of the box, towards the outside of the box. This will help reduce the chances of leaving sharp edges inside the cage, which could cut the snake.

If you intend to heat a single plastic storage box with a heat lamp, you will need to cut a hole in the lid, and cover the hole with hardware cloth or screen. Attach the mesh or hardware cloth with silicone or cable ties. You can now place the heat lamp on top of the mesh.

Homemade Cages

For keepers with access to tools and the desire and skill to use them, it is possible to construct homemade cages.

A number of materials are suitable for cage construction, and each has different pros and cons. Wood is commonly used, but must be adequately sealed to avoid rotting, warping or absorbing offensive odors.

Plastic sheeting is a very good material, but few have the necessary skills, knowledge and tools necessary for cage construction. Additionally, some plastics may have extended off-gassing times.

Glass can be used, whether glued to itself or when used with a frame. Custom-built glass cages can be better than aquariums, as you can design them in dimensions that are appropriate for snakes. Additionally, they can be constructed in such a way that the door is on the front of the cage, rather than the top.

Security and safety are of paramount importance when constructing a custom cage.

Screen Cages
Screen cages make excellent habitats for some lizards and frogs, but they are not suitable for green tree pythons. Screened cages do not retain heat well, and they are hard to keep suitably humid. Additionally, they are difficult to clean. Screen cages are prone to developing week spots that can give the inhabitant enough of a hole to push through and escape.

2) Temperature

Providing the proper thermal environment is one of the most important aspects of snake husbandry. As ectothermic ("cold blooded") animals, snakes rely on the local temperatures to regulate the rate at which their metabolism operates. Providing a proper thermal environment can mean the difference between keeping your pet healthy and spending your time at the veterinarian's office, battling infections and illness.

In general, green tree pythons prefer temperatures in the high-70s to mid-80s Fahrenheit (about 25 to 31 degrees Celsius). At night, chondros safely tolerate temperatures in the high-60s Fahrenheit (about 20 degrees Celsius).

In their natural range, green tree pythons are seldom exposed to temperatures outside this range, so they do not exhibit the drastic thermoregulatory habits of snakes from less hospitable environments.

3) Thermal Gradients

In the wild, pythons move between different microhabitats so that they can maintain ideal body temperature as much as possible. You want to provide similar opportunities for captive snakes by creating a thermal gradient.

To establish a thermal gradient, place the heating devices at one end of the habitat. This creates a basking spot, which should have the highest temperatures in the cage – around between 90 degrees Fahrenheit (32 degrees Celsius). This area should be equal to the size of your snake's coiled body so that he can warm his entire body if necessary.

Because there is no heat source at the other end of the cage, the temperature will gradually fall as your snake moves away from the heat source.

Ideally, the difference between the coolest spot in the cage and the basking spot will be at least 12 to 14 Fahrenheit (8 to 10 degrees Celsius), and larger if possible. If more than one heat source is required for the habitat, they should be clustered at one end.

The need to establish a thermal gradient is one of the most compelling reasons to use a large cage. In general, the larger the cage, the easier it is to establish a suitable thermal gradient.

4) Heat Lamps

Heat lamps are one of the best choices for supplying heat to green tree pythons. Heat lamps consist of a reflector dome and an incandescent bulb. The light bulb produces heat (in addition to light) and the metal reflector dome directs the heat to a spot inside the cage.

If you use a cage with a metal screen lid, you can rest the reflector dome directly on the screen; otherwise, you will need to clamp the lamp to something over the cage. Always be sure that the lamp is securely attached and will not be dislodged by vibration, children or pets. Always opt to purchase heavy-duty reflector domes with ceramic bases, rather than economy units with plastic bases.

While you can use specialized light bulbs that are designed for use with reptiles, it is not necessary. Regular, economy, incandescent bulbs work well. Snakes do not require special lighting; incandescent bulbs – even those produced for use with reptiles – rarely generate much UVA, and they never generate UVB.

One of the greatest benefits of using heat lamps to maintain the temperature of your snake's habitat is the flexibility. While heat tapes and other devices are easy to adjust, you need a rheostat or thermostat to do so. Such devices are not prohibitively expensive, but they will raise the budget of your snake's habitat.

By contrast, heat lamps offer flexibility in two ways:

Changing the Bulb Wattage

The simplest way to adjust the temperature of your green tree python's cage is by changing the wattage of the bulb you are using.

For example, if a 40-watt light bulb is not raising the temperature of the basking spot high enough, you may try a 60-watt bulb. Alternatively, if a 100-watt light bulb is elevating the cage temperatures higher than are appropriate, switching to a 60-watt bulb may help.

Adjusting the Height of the Heat Lamp

The closer the heat lamp is to the cage, the warmer the cage will be. If the habitat is too warm, you can raise the light, which should lower the cage temperatures slightly.

However, the higher you raise the lamp, the larger the basking spot becomes. It is important to be careful that you do not raise the light too high, which results in reducing the effectiveness of the cage's thermal gradient. In very large cages, this may not compromise the thermal gradient very much, but in a small cage, it may eliminate the "cool side" of the habitat.

In other words, if your heat lamp creates a basking spot that is roughly 1-foot in diameter when it rests directly on the screen, it may produce a slightly cooler, but larger basking spot when raised 6-inches above the level of the screen.

One way to avoid reducing the effectiveness of the gradient is through the use of "spot" bulbs, which produce a relatively narrow beam of light. Such lights may be slightly more expensive than economy bulbs, but because they make heat gradients easier to achieve, they deserve consideration.

One problem with using heat lamps is that many manufacturers have stopped producing incandescent bulbs. In some municipalities, they may even be illegal to sell. It remains to be seen if incandescent bulbs will remain available to herpetoculturists over the long term or not. Fortunately, many other heating options are available.

5) Ceramic Heat Emitters

Ceramic heat emitters are small inserts that function as light bulbs do, except that they do not produce any visible light – they only produce heat.

Ceramic heat emitters are used in reflector-dome fixtures, just as heat lamps are. The benefits of such devices are numerous:

- They typically last much longer than light bulbs do
- They are suitable for use with thermostats
- They allow for the creation of overhead basking spots
- They can be used day or night

However, the devices do have three primary drawbacks:

- They are very hot when in operation
- They are much more expensive than light bulbs
- You cannot tell by looking if they are hot or cool. This can be a safety hazard – touching a ceramic heat emitter while it is hot is likely to cause serious burns.

Ceramic heat emitters are much less expensive than radiant heat panels are. This causes many to select them instead of radiant heat panels. However, radiant heat panels are generally preferable to ceramic heat emitters, as they usually have a light that indicates when they are on, and they do not get as hot on the surface.

6) Radiant Heat Panels

Quality radiant heat panels are the best choice for heating most reptile habitats, including those containing green tree pythons. Radiant heat panels are essentially heat pads that stick to the roof of the habitat. They usually feature rugged, plastic or metal casings and internal reflectors to direct the infrared heat back into the cage.

Radiant heat panels have a number of benefits over traditional heat lamps and under tank heat pads:

- They do not contact the animal at all, thus reducing the risk of burns.
- They do not produce visible light, which means they are useful for both diurnal and nocturnal heat production. They can be used in conjunction with fluorescent light fixtures during the day, and remain on at night once the lights go off.
- They are inherently flexible. Unlike many devices that do not work well with pulse-proportional thermostats, most radiant heat panels work well with on-off and pulse-proportional thermostats.

The only real drawback to radiant heat panels is their cost: radiant heat panels often cost about two to three times the price of light- or heat pad-oriented systems. However, many radiant heat panels outlast light bulbs and heat pads, which offsets their high initial cost.

7) Heat Pads

Heat pads are an attractive option for many new keepers, but they are not without drawbacks.

- Heat pads have a high risk for causing contact burns.
- If they malfunction, they can damage the cage as well as the surface on which they are placed.
- They are more likely to cause a fire than heat lamps or radiant heat panels are.
- They are not ideal for arboreal species.

However, if installed properly (which includes allowing fresh air to flow over the exposed side of the heat pad) and used in conjunction with a thermostat, they can be reasonably safe. With heat pads, it behooves the keeper to purchase premium products, despite the small increase in price.

8) Heat Tape

Heat tape is somewhat akin to "stripped down" heat pads. In fact, most heat pads are simply pieces of heat tape that have already been connected and sealed inside a plastic envelope. Heat tape is primarily used to heat large numbers of cages simultaneously. It is generally inappropriate for novices, and requires the keeper to make electrical connections. Additionally, a thermostat is always required when using heat tape.

Historically, heat tape was used to keep water pipes from freezing – not to heat reptile cages. While some commercial heat tapes have been designed specifically for reptiles, many have not. Accordingly, it may be illegal, not to mention dangerous, to use heat tapes for purposes other than for which they are designed.

9) Heat Cables

Heat cables are similar to heat tape, in that they heat a long strip of the cage, but they are much more flexible and easy to use. Many heat cables are suitable to use inside the cage, while others are designed for use outside the habitat.

Always be sure to purchase heat cables that are designed to be used in reptile cages. Those sold at hardware stores are not appropriate for use in a cage.

Heat cables must be used in conjunction with a thermostat, or, at the very least, a rheostat.

10) Hot Rocks

In the early days of commercial reptile products, faux rocks, branches and caves with internal heating elements were very popular. However, they have generally fallen out of favor among modern keepers. These rocks and branches were often made with poor craftsmanship and cheap materials, causing them to fail and produce tragic results. Additionally, many keepers used the rocks improperly, leading to injuries, illnesses and death for many unfortunate reptiles.

These types of heat sources are not designed to heat an entire cage; they are designed to provide a localized source of heat for the reptile. Nevertheless, many keepers tried to use them as the primary heat source for the cage, resulting in dangerously cool cage temperatures.

When snakes must rely on small, localized heat sources placed in otherwise chilly cages, they often hug these heat sources for extended periods of time. This can lead to serious thermal burns – whether or not the units function properly. This illustrates the key reason why these devices make adequate supplemental heat sources, but they should not be used as primary heating sources.

Modern hot rocks and branches utilize better features, materials and craftsmanship than the old models did, but they still offer few benefits to the keeper or the kept. Additionally, any heating devices that are designed to be used inside the cage necessitate passing an electric cable through a hole, which is not always easy to accomplish. However, some cages do feature passageways for chords.

11) Thermometers

It is important to monitor the cage temperatures very carefully to ensure your pet stays health. Just as a water test kit is an aquarist's best friend, a quality thermometer is one of the most important husbandry tools for snakes.

Ambient and Surface Temperatures
Two different types of temperature are relevant for pet snakes: ambient temperatures and surface temperatures.

The ambient temperature in your animal's cage is the air temperature. By contrast, surface temperatures are the temperatures of the objects in the cage.

For example, the air temperatures may be 90 degrees Fahrenheit (32 degrees Celsius) on a hot summer day. However, the surface of a black rock may be much hotter than this. If you checked the surface temperatures of the rock, it may be in excess of 120 degrees Fahrenheit (48 degrees Celsius).

In general, the ambient temperatures require more frequent monitoring and attention. As long as the surface temperatures of the cage do not exceed about 120 degrees Fahrenheit, your snake is not likely to be harmed from incidental contact. However, ambient temperatures of 120 degrees would be fatal very quickly.

Measure the cage's ambient temperatures with a digital thermometer. An indoor-outdoor model will feature a probe that allows you to measure the temperature at both ends of the thermal gradient at once. For example, you may position the thermometer at the cool side of the cage, but place the remote probe under the basking lamp.

Standard digital thermometers do not measure surface temperatures well. Instead, you should use a non-contact, infrared thermometer. Such devices will allow you to measure surface temperatures accurately and from a short distance away.

12) Thermostats and Rheostats

Some heating devices, such as heat lamps, are designed to operate at full capacity for the entire time that they are turned on. Such devices should not be used with thermostats – instead, care should be taken to calibrate the proper temperature by tweaking the bulb wattage.

Other devices, such as heat pads, heat tape and radiant heat panels are designed to be used with a regulating device, such as a thermostat or rheostat, which maintains the proper temperature

Rheostats

Rheostats are similar to light-dimmer switches, and they allow you to reduce the output of a heating device. In this way, you can dial in the proper temperature for the habitat.

The drawback to rheostats is that they only regulate the amount of power going to the device – they do not monitor the cage temperature or adjust the power flow automatically. In practice, even with the same level of power entering the device, the amount of heat generated by most heat sources will vary over the course of the day.

If you set the rheostat so that it keeps the cage at the right temperature in the morning, it may become too hot by the middle of the day. Conversely, setting the proper temperature during the middle of the day may leave the morning temperatures too cool.

Care must be taken to ensure that the rheostat controller is not inadvertently bumped or jostled, causing the temperature to rise or fall outside of healthy parameters.

Thermostats

Thermostats are similar to rheostats, except that they also feature a temperature probe that monitors the temperature in the cage (or under the basking source). This allows the thermostat to adjust the power going to the device as necessary to maintain a predetermined temperature.

For example, if you place the temperature probe under a basking spot powered by a radiant heat panel, the thermostat will keep the temperature relatively constant under the basking site.

There are two different types of thermostats:

- On-Off Thermostats work by cutting the power to the device when the probe's temperature reaches a given temperature. For example, if the thermostat were set to 85 degrees Fahrenheit (29 degrees Celsius), the heating device would turn off whenever the temperature exceeds this threshold. When the temperature falls below 85, the thermostat restores power to the unit, and the heater begins functioning again. This cycle will continue to repeat, thus maintaining the temperature within a relatively small range.

  Be aware that on-off thermostats have a "lag" factor, meaning that they do not turn off when the temperature reaches a given temperature. They turn off when the temperature is a few degrees *above* that temperature, and then turn back on when the temperate is a little *below* the set point. Because of this, it is important to avoid setting the temperature at the limits of your pet's acceptable range. Some premium models have an adjustable amount of threshold for this factor, which is helpful.

- Pulse proportional thermostats work by constantly sending pulses of electricity to the heater. By varying the rate of pulses, the amount of energy reaching the heating devices varies. A small computer inside the thermostat adjusts this rate to match the set-point temperature as measured by the probe. Accordingly, pulse proportional thermostats maintain much more consistent temperatures than on-off thermostats do.

Lights should not be used with thermostats, as the constant flickering may stress your snake. Conversely, heat pads, heat tape, radiant heat panels and ceramic heat emitters should always be used with either a rheostat or, preferably, a thermostat to avoid overheating your snake.

Thermostat Failure

If used for long enough, all thermostats eventually fail. The question is will yours fail today or twenty years from now. While some thermostats fail in the "off" position, a thermostat that fails in the "on" position may overheat your snakes. Unfortunately, tales of entire collections being lost to a faulty thermostat are too common.

Accordingly, it behooves the keeper to acquire high-quality thermostats. Some keepers use two thermostats, connected in series arrangement. By setting the second thermostat (the "backup thermostat") a few degrees higher than the setting used on the "primary thermostat," you safeguard yourself against the failure of either unit.

In such a scenario, the backup thermostat allows the full power coming to it to travel through to the heating device, as the temperature never reaches its higher set-point temperature.

However, if the first unit fails in the "on" position, the second thermostat will keep the temperatures from rising too high. The temperature will rise a few degrees in accordance with the higher set-point temperature, but it will not get hot enough to harm your snakes.

If the backup thermostat fails in the "on" position, the first thermostat retains control. If either fails in the "off" position, the temperature will fall until you rectify the situation, but a brief exposure to relatively cool temperatures is unlikely to be fatal.

13) Nighttime Heating

In most circumstances, you should provide your green tree python with a minor temperature drop at night. Some keepers have success by providing constant heat, but wild green tree pythons experience day-night temperature fluctuations, which may provide some benefits.

If your home does not dip far below 68 degrees Fahrenheit (20 degrees Celsius) at night, you can simply switch your heating device off at night, and turn it back on in the morning.

Alternatively, you can plug the heating devices (and thermostats or rheostats) into a lamp-timer to automate the process. Some thermostats even have features that adjust the temperature of the thermostat during the night, lowering it to a specified level.

Others, who must provide some type of nocturnal heat source for their pet, can do so in a number of ways. Virtually any non-light-emitting heat source will function adequately in this capacity. Ceramic heating elements, radiant heat panels and heat pads, cables and tape all work well for supplying nocturnal heat.

Red lights can be used in reflector domes to provide heat as well. In fact, red lights can be used for heating during the day and night, but the cage will not be illuminated very well, unless other lights are incorporated during the day.

14) Incorporating Thermal Mass

One underutilized technique that is helpful for raising the temperature of a cage is to increase the cage's thermal mass.

Rocks, large water dishes and ceramic cage decorations are examples of items that may work in such contexts. These objects will absorb heat from the heat source, and then re-radiate heat into the habitat.

This changes the thermal characteristics of the habitat greatly. Often, keepers in cool climates benefit from these techniques when trying to warm cages sufficiently. By simply adding a large rock, the cage may eventually warm up a few degrees.

Raising the cage's thermal mass also helps to reduce the cage's rate of cooling in the evening. By placing a thick rock under the basking light, it will absorb heat all day and radiate this heat after the lights turn off. Eventually it will reach room temperature, but this may take hours.

Always remember to monitor the cage surface temperatures and ambient temperatures regularly after changing the thermal characteristics of the cage. Pay special attention to the surface temperatures of items placed on or under a heat source.

Experiment with different amounts of thermal mass in the cage. Use items of different sizes, shapes and materials, and see how the cage temperatures change. In general, the more thermal mass in the cage, the more constant the temperature will stay.

15) Room Heat

Some keepers with very large collections elect to heat the entire room, rather than individual cages. While this is an economic and viable solution for advanced keepers, it is not appropriate for novices.

Heating the whole room, instead of an individual cage, makes it very difficult to achieve a good thermal gradient. Experienced keepers may be able to maintain their snakes successfully in this manner, but beginners should always rely on the added safety afforded by a gradient.

Additionally, room heat is rarely cost-effective for a keeper with a pet snake or two. Relying on a single heating source for an entire room is also a high-risk proposition; if the heater or thermostat fails in the "on" position, the entire room may overheat.

16) Lights

Green tree pythons do not require special or elaborate lighting. Heat lamps provide plenty of illumination for them, while ambient light that enters their cage is sufficient for cages that do not use heat lamps. However, some keepers prefer to incorporate supplemental lighting to improve the visibility of their snakes.

Fluorescent bulbs are the best choice for supplemental lighting. These lights produce higher quality light than incandescent bulbs do, and they do not produce very much heat.

Full-spectrum lights with a high color-rendering index will make your snake look his best, but even economy bulbs will allow you to see your animal better. Reptile-specific lights are not required for green tree pythons, as they do not require exposure to ultraviolet radiation to metabolize their dietary calcium and vitamin D, as many lizards and turtles do.

Always measure the cage temperatures after adding or changing the type of light sources used. While fluorescent lights do not produce a lot of heat, they may generate enough to warm small cages to undesirable levels.

17) Substrate

Substrates are used to give your snake a comfortable surface on which to crawl and to absorb any liquids present. There are a variety of acceptable choices, all of which have benefits and drawbacks. The only common substrate that is never acceptable is cedar shavings, which emits fumes that are toxic to snakes.

Paper Products
The easiest and safest substrates for green tree pythons are paper products in sheet form. While regular newspaper is the most common choice, some keepers prefer paper towels, unprinted newspaper, butcher's paper or a commercial version of these products.

Paper substrates are very easy to maintain, but they do not last very long. You must replace them completely when they are soiled. Accordingly, they must be changed regularly -- at least once per week.

Use several layers of paper products to provide sufficient absorbency and a little bit of cushion for the snake.

Aspen
Shredded aspen bark is a popular substrate choice for many snakes, but it is not ideal for chondros. Aspen decomposes rapidly when it gets wet, and it is not a good substrate for high-humidity cages.

Pine
Pine shavings are similar to aspen shavings. Besides being unsuitable for humid cages, pine shavings are very aromatic. Some keepers worry that the fumes from pine shavings may be toxic to snakes. While this has yet to be conclusively demonstrated, it is quite possible. The best course of action is to err on the side of caution, and avoid pine shavings.

By contrast, pine bark mulch is a reasonable substrate for green tree pythons. The bark from pine trees is not particularly aromatic and contains no sap. Additionally, pine bark mulch resists decay for longer than mulch made from the wood of the trees, although it eventually does breakdown in damp conditions.

Orchid Bark
The bark of fir trees is often used for orchid propagation, and so it is often called "orchid bark." Orchid bark is very attractive, though not quite as natural looking as pine bark. However, it exceeds pine in most other ways except cost.

Orchid bark absorbs water very well, so keepers who maintain rainforest species often use it. Additionally, orchid bark is easy to spot clean. However, monthly replacement can be expensive for those living in the Eastern United States and Europe.

Cypress Mulch

Cypress mulch is a popular substrate choice for many tropical species. It looks attractive and holds humidity well. However, some brands (or individual bags among otherwise good brands) produce a stick-like mulch, rather than mulch composed of thicker pieces.

These sharp sticks can injure the keeper and the kept. It usually only takes one cypress mulch splinter jammed under a keeper's fingernail to cause them to switch substrates.

Pulp Products

Many commercial pulp products have become available over the last decade. Comprised of recycled wood fibers, these products are very absorbent, but pose an ingestion hazard as they may swell once inside a snake's digestive system.

Nevertheless, many keepers prefer pulp products to all other substrates. If these types of substrate are used, care should be taken to ensure the snakes do not swallow any of the substrate.

These products often absorb odors and liquids well, but with proper cage hygiene, snake cages should not emit objectionable odors.

Water

Many years ago, when green tree python husbandry was still in its infancy, some keepers experimented with keeping their green tree python over a pool of water. Effectively, they used water as a substrate.

The thinking was that this method would help raise the humidity of the cage and allow for easy cleaning. However, experience has shown that it is very labor intensive to keep the water adequately clean. In general, this option is ill advised.

Substrate Comparison Chart

Substrate	Pros	Cons
Newspaper	Safe, low-cost, and easy to maintain.	Not very attractive.. Cannot be spot-cleaned.
Paper Towels	Safe and easy to maintain.	Not very attractive. Cannot be spot-cleaned.
Commercial Paper Product	Safe and easy to maintain.	Not very attractive. Can be expensive with long term use. Cannot be spot-cleaned.
Aspen Shavings	Easy to spot clean.	May be ingested, messy, can be expensive. Rots if it becomes wet.
Pine Bark Mulch	Attractive and easy to spot clean.	May be ingested, messy, can be expensive.
Cypress Mulch	Attractive and easy to spot clean. Retains moisture well.	May be ingested, sharp sticks may harm snakes, messy, can be expensive.
Fir (Orchid) Bark	Attractive and easy to spot clean. Retains moisture well.	May be ingested, messy, can be expensive.
Pulp Paper Products	Easy to spot-clean.	Not very attractive. May be ingested, messy, can be expensive.

18) Cage Furniture

Chondros require very little cage furniture. The only items that are necessary are a suitable perch and a water bowl. Unlike most other commonly kept snakes, green tree pythons do not require hide boxes.

Nevertheless, you can place other items in your green tree python's cage, such as live or artificial plants. While such measures are not necessary, they often make the cage look better, and provide your snake with some security.

However, it is recommended that beginners keep things simple for the first 6 to 12 months while they learn to provide effective husbandry.

19) Climbing Branches

Healthy green tree pythons spend the majority of their time wrapped around their perches. Accordingly, it is important to provide them with a perch that makes them feel comfortable.

You must provide your snake with at least one perch, but it is better to offer multiple perches. This will help encourage activity and exercise, as well as provide your snake with multiple perching locations.

Acquiring and Preparing Perches
You can purchase climbing branches from pet and craft stores, or you can collect them yourself. When collecting your own branches, try to use branches that are still attached to trees (always obtain permission first). Such branches are less likely to harbor insects or other invertebrate pests than fallen, dead branches will.

Most of the insects that infest wood will cause your snake no harm, but they may scatter frass (insect droppings mixed with wood shavings) throughout the cage, causing the keeper more work. Theoretically, some of these insects may be damaging to your house, should they escape the cage.

It is always advisable to sterilize branches before placing them in a cage. The easiest way to do so is by placing the branch in a 300-degree oven for about 15 minutes. Doing so should kill the vast majority of pests and pathogens lurking inside the wood.

Some keepers like to cover their branches with a water-sealing product. This is acceptable if a non-toxic product is used and the branches are allowed to air dry for several days before being placed in the cage. However, as branches are relatively easy and inexpensive to replace, it is not necessary to seal them if you plan to replace them.

Attaching Perches to the Enclosure

You can attach the branches to the cage walls in many different ways. The branches should be held very securely, but you must be able to remove them when necessary. Instead of picking your green tree python up, simply lift the entire branch out, snake and all.

Closet rod holders are a popular choice, but they must not allow the branches to roll when the snake climbs on them. To keep them in a fixed position, small pegs can be placed on the branch ends that prevent them from rolling. Alternatively, branches with three or more ends can be used; three or more contact points prevent the branch from spinning.

Some keepers use hooks and eye-screws to suspend their branches. This method allows for quick and easy removal, but it is only applicable for cages with walls that will accept and support the eye-screws.

It can be challenging to suspend branches in glass cages and aquaria. It is often necessary to use an adhesive to hold the supports securely to the cage walls. This can be a problem if the adhesive loses strength and fails with your snake on top of it.

Another option is to make self-supporting structures for your green tree python to climb. Many branches can be placed in cages in such a way that they will support themselves. Use complex branches and trim them to fit the glass habitat. Usually, a large part of the branch should be on the cage floor to support its weight. Be careful placing pressure on glass walls or panels, as they crack easily.

Many different types of branches can be used in green tree python cages. Most non-aromatic hardwoods suffice. See the chart below for specific recommendations.

Whenever collecting wood to be used as cage props, bring a ruler so that you can visualize how large the branch will be, once it is back in the cage. Leave several inches of spare material at each end of the branch; this way, you can cut the perch to the correct length, once you arrive back home.

Always wash branches with plenty of hot water and a stiff, metal-bristled scrub brush to remove as much dirt, dust and fungus as possible before placing them in your chondro's cage. Clean stubborn spots with a little bit of dish soap, but be sure to rinse them thoroughly afterwards.

Snakes That Will Not Perch
Occasionally, green tree pythons fail to utilize their perches. Others may spend most of their time perched, but descend to the ground and stay there for a few days. While this is no cause for concern in healthy animals, it can signify that the snake is ill or the temperatures are too warm.

- Use branches of many different diameters. Most green tree pythons prefer perches that are about the size of their body, or slightly smaller.
- Place the branches so that they are as close to horizontal as possible.
- Be sure to attach the branches to the cage wall securely, so the branches do not shift or rotate on their axis. Green tree pythons do not like to perch on branches that do not feel stable.
- Try to provide several different branches for your snake to spread his weight across.

Recommended Tree Species for Perches

Recommended Species	Species to Avoid
Maple trees (*Acer* spp.)	**Cherry trees** (*Prunus* spp.)
Oak trees (*Quercus* spp.)	**Pine trees** (*Pinus* spp.)
Walnut trees *(Juglans* spp.)	**Cedar trees** (*Cedrus* spp., etc.)
Ash trees (*Fraxinus* spp.)	**Juniper trees** (*Juniperus* spp.)
Dogwood trees (*Cornus* spp.)	**Poison ivy / oak** (*Toxicodendron* spp.)
Sweetgum trees (*Liquidambar stryaciflua*)	
Crepe Myrtle trees (Lagerstroemia spp.)	
Tuliptrees (*Liriodendron tulipifera*)	
Pear trees (*Pyrus* spp.)	
Apple trees (*Malus* spp.)	
Manzanitas (*Arctostaphylos* spp.) **Grapevine** (*Vitis* spp.)	

Green tree pythons prefer horizontal branches, but they can rest comfortably on diagonal branches as well.

Chapter 6: Maintaining the Captive Habitat

1) Cleaning Procedures

Once you have decided on the proper cage for your pet, you must keep your snake fed, hydrated and ensure that the habitat stays in proper working order. This will require you to examine the cage daily to ensure that your snake is healthy and comfortable.

Some tasks must be completed each day, while others are should be performed weekly, monthly or annually.

Daily
- Monitor the ambient and surface temperatures of the habitat.
- Ensure that the snake's water bowl is full of clean water.
- Ensure that the snake has not defecated or produced urates in the cage. If he has, you must clean the cage.
- Ensure that the lights, latches and other moving parts are in working order.
- Verify that your snake is acting normally and appears healthy. You do not need to handle him to do so.
- Ensure that the humidity and ventilation are at appropriate levels.

Weekly
- Feed your snake (this may not be necessary each week).
- Empty, wash and refill the water container.
- Change any sheet-like substrate.
- Clean the walls of the enclosure.
- Remove your snake (you can remove the perch with the snake if your snake is not easily handled) and inspect him for any injuries, parasites or signs of illness.

Monthly

- Break down the cage completely, remove and discard the substrate.
- Clean the entire cage from top to bottom.
- Sterilize the water dish and any other plastic or ceramic furniture in a mild bleach solution.
- Measure and weigh your snake (if your snake is not easy to handle, note the weight of his perch so that you can weigh him without removing him from the perch in the future).
- Soak your snake for about 1 hour (Recommended, but not imperative).
- Photograph your snake (Recommended, but not imperative).

Annually

- Visit the veterinarian to ensure that your snake is in good health.
- Replace the batteries in your thermometers and any other devices that use them.

Cleaning a snake's cage or an item from his cage is relatively simple. Regardless of the way it became soiled or its constituent materials, the basic process is the same:

1. Rinse the object
2. Using a scrub brush or sponge and soapy water, remove any organic debris from the object.
3. Rinse the object thoroughly.
4. Disinfect the object.
5. Re-rinse the object.
6. Dry the object.

2) Chemicals & Tools

A variety of chemicals and tools are necessary for snake care. Save yourself some time by purchasing dedicated cleaning products and keeping them in the same place that you keep your tools.

Scrub Brushes or Sponges

It helps to have a few different types of scrub brushes, sponges and similar tools. Use the least abrasive sponge or brush suitable for the task to prevent wearing out cage items prematurely. Do not use abrasive materials on glass or acrylic surfaces. Steel-bristled brushes work well for scrubbing wooden items, such as branches.

Spatulas and Putty Knives

Spatulas, putty knives and similar tools are often helpful for cleaning snake cages. For example, urates often become stuck on cage walls or furniture. The best way to remove them is by scraping them with a sturdy plastic putty knife.

Small Vacuums

Small, handheld vacuums are very helpful for sucking up the dust left behind from substrates. They are also helpful for cleaning the tracks that hold sliding glass cage doors. A shop vacuum, with suitable hoses and attachments, can also be helpful.

Steam Cleaners

Steam cleaners are very effective for sterilizing cages, water bowls and durable cage props after they have been cleaned. Steam is a very effective for sterilizing surfaces, and it will not leave behind a toxic residue. Never use a steam cleaner near your snake or any other living creatures.

Soap

Use gentle, non-scented dish soap. Antibacterial soap is preferred, but not necessary. Most people use far more soap than is necessary -- a few drops mixed with a quantity of water is usually sufficient to help remove surface pollutants.

Bleach

Bleach (diluted to one-half cup per gallon of water) makes an excellent disinfectant. Be careful not to spill any on clothing, carpets or furniture, as it is likely to discolor the objects. Soak water bowls in this type of dilute bleach solution monthly.

Always be sure to rinse objects thoroughly after using bleach and be sure that you cannot detect any residual odor. Bleach does not work as a disinfectant when in contact with organic substances; accordingly, the cage must be cleaned before you can disinfect it.

Veterinarian Approved Disinfectant
Many commercial products are available that are designed to be safe for their pets. Consult with your veterinarian about the best product for your situation, its method of use and its proper dilution.

Avoid Phenols
Always avoid cleaners that contain phenols, as they are extremely toxic to snakes. In general, do not use household cleaning products to avoid exposing your pet to toxic chemicals.

3) Keeping Records

It is important to keep records regarding your snake's health, feeding, shedding and other important details. In the past, snake keepers would do so on small index cards or in a notebook. In the modern world, technological solutions may be easier, such as using your computer or mobile device to keep track of the pertinent info about your snake.

There is no limit to the amount of information you can record about your snake – and the more information to you record, the better. At a minimum, you should record the following:

Pedigree and Origin Information
Be sure to record the source of your pet, the date on which you acquired him and any other data that is available. If you purchase the snake from a quality breeder, you will likely be provided with information regarding the sire, dam, date of birth, weights and feeding records for the snake's entire life thus far.

Feeding Information

At a minimum, record the date and type of food item your snake eats at each feeding. If possible, record the time of day and weight of the food item as well. Additional notes may include techniques that were or were not successful, the prey species, and the color of the prey or any scenting techniques used. It is also helpful to record refused meals as well.

Shedding Information

It is only necessary to record the date of each shed, but it may also be helpful to record the date you notice the snake's eyes turning blue (although this is often difficult to notice in green tree pythons). Additionally, be sure to note any shedding difficulties. If you have to take steps to rectify a bad shed, note these as well.

Weights and Length

At a minimum, you should record the weight of your snake monthly or each time he sheds. Because you look at your snake frequently, it is difficult to determine his growth rate visually. It is important to track his weight to ensure he is growing properly.

If you like, you can measure his length as well, but doing so is very difficult to produce accurate results. There are computer programs that will calculate the length of your snake if you photograph him near a ruler.

Maintenance Information

Record the dates and details of any major maintenance. For example, while it is not necessary to note that you topped off the water dish each day, it is appropriate to record the dates on which you changed the substrate, or sterilized the cage.

Whenever you purchase new equipment, supplies or caging, note the date and source. This not only helps to remind you when you purchased the items, but it may help you track down a source for the items in the future, if necessary.

Breeding Information

If you intend on breeding your snake, you should record all details regarding the pre-breeding conditioning, cycling, introductions, copulations, ovulation, post-ovulation shed and egg deposition.

Record all pertinent information about the clutch as well, including the number of viable eggs, as well as the number of unhatched and unfertilized eggs (often called "slugs" by snake keepers).

Record Keeping Samples
The following are two different examples of suitable recording systems. The first example is reminiscent of the style of card that many breeders and experienced hobbyists use. Because such keepers often have numerous snakes, the notes are very simple, and require a minimum amount of writing or typing.

Note that in this example, the keeper has employed a simple code, so that he or she does not have to write out "fed this snake one small, thawed mouse."

ID Number: 44522	Genus: Species/Sub:	Morelia viridis	Gender: DOB:	Male 3/20/13	CARD #2
6.30.13 HM	7.07.13 HM	7.30.13 HM	8.06.13 SM	8.24.13 SM	
7.01.13 SHED	7.14.13 HM	8.02.13 REFUSED HM	8.13.13 SM	8.30.13 SM	
7.04.13 HM	7.21.13 HM	8.05.13 SHED	8.20.13 SM		
FM= Fuzzy Mouse	HM= Hopper Mouse	SM = Small Mouse	LM = Large Mouse		

The second example demonstrates a simple approach that is employed by many novice keepers – keeping notes on paper. Such notes could be taken in a notebook or journal, or simply typed into a word processor. It does not ultimately matter *how* you keep records, just that you *do* keep records.

Date	Notes
6-22-13	*Acquired ""Verdi" the green tree python from a snake breeder named Mark at the in-town reptile expo. Mark explained that Verdi's scientific name is Morelia viridis. Cost was $325. Mark was not sure what sex Monty was, as he did not like to probe the young snakes. Mark said the snake hatched in March, but he does not know the exact date.*
6-23-13	*I have decided to consider Verdi a boy until he gets big enough to probe. Verdi spent the night in the container I bought him in. I purchased a 20-gallon aquarium, screened lid and heat lamp at the pet store. Bought the thermometer at the hardware store next door and ordered a non-contact thermometer online. I am using old food containers for his water dish. I bought some fake vines at the pet store to make his perches.*
6-27-13	*Verdi shed today! He looks beautiful. Everything came off in one long piece.*
6-30-13	*I fed Verdi a thawed hopper mouse today. I think I need longer tweezers! He was hungry!*
7-1-13	*Since Verdi looked so hungry, I fed him another thawed mouse today.*
7-8-13	*Fed Verdi one mouse. This one was brown, instead of white, but he didn't seem to care.*

2) Common Husbandry Problems and Solutions

Problem	Solution
Cage too cool	• Increase power / wattage of heating devices • Add additional heating devices • Place heating devices closer to the cage • Incorporate more thermal mass in the cage • Insulate the cage • Reduce the ventilation slightly • Move the cage to a different location
Cage too warm	• Reduce power / wattage of heating devices • Remove some of the heating devices • Use a rheostat / thermostat to reduce temperature • Remove thermal mass from the cage • Move cage to a different location
Cage too dry	• Mist the cage more frequently / thoroughly • Increase the size of the water dish • Use moisture-retaining substrate • Reduce ventilation slightly • Add live plants to the enclosure • Use bubbler in water dish
Cage too damp	• Increase ventilation • Swap live plants for artificial plants • Reduce the size of the water dish • Allow substrate to dry before adding to the cage

Problem	Solution
Incomplete sheds	<ul><li>Increase cage humidity</li><li>Include a humid hide box</li><li>Implement a soaking regimen</li><li>Avoid handling snake during shed cycles</li><li>Ensure the snake has no health problems (mites, etc.)</li></ul>
Snake doesn't eat	<ul><li>Try feeding at a different time of day</li><li>Experiment with different food items (mice, chicks, rats)</li><li>Experiment with different food presentations</li><li>Assess cage temperatures, ensure they are correct</li><li>Reduce the snake's stress -- less handling, more privacy</li></ul>
Snake cage smells	<ul><li>Clean the cage more often / thoroughly</li><li>Switch to paper substrate</li><li>Increase cage ventilation</li></ul>
Snake pacing cage	<ul><li>Ensure cage temperatures are not too high</li><li>Ensure snake has water</li><li>Ensure the snake has an adequate number of hides</li><li>Mature males may be searching for female</li></ul>
Snake is aggressive	<ul><li>Ensure the cage is not subject to vibration, etc.</li></ul>

- Ensure the cage features enough hiding opportunities
- Ensure temperatures are correct
- Reduce handling frequency

Chapter 7: Feeding Green Tree Pythons

Green tree pythons are obligate carnivores that consume a wide variety of prey in the wild.

1) Live, Fresh Killed or Frozen

Whenever possible, snakes should be fed dead prey. Most often, this comes in the form of frozen-thawed rodents.

While green tree pythons are perfectly capable of killing and consuming small rodents, birds or lizards, these animals often fight back. If the snake does not grab its prey correctly, the creature may be free enough to bite or scratch the snake. Such bites can cause serious injuries to snakes, especially if they occur on the snake's head.

Additionally, it is far more humane for prey animal to be humanely euthanized than it is to be bitten, constricted and eaten by a snake.

Whenever thawing rodents, do so in warm water or at room temperature. Never attempt to thaw a rodent in the microwave.

This green tree python is exhibiting the species' classic ambush posture.

2) Prey Species

In most circumstances, green tree pythons should be fed commercially raised rodents. However, some keepers prefer to feed their snakes captive produced chicks or ducks.

Some hobbyists strive to feed their snake a combination of birds and rodents. While alternating between rodents and birds may provide some small health benefits, many generations of snakes have been successfully raised solely on a diet of lab-raised rodents.

Snakes that eat birds often produce soft, offensive smelling feces. Additionally, the chance of birds transmitting salmonella to your snakes is higher than it is with most other food sources.

3) Prey Size

Green tree pythons can consume relatively large prey, but it is usually best to provide them with moderate-sized food items.

Unlike Burmese pythons (Python bivittatus) who may consume prey representing half their body weight, green tree pythons do best when fed food that is about the same diameter as the snake's body is. This is important because a Burmese python may crawl in a burrow and sleep for a month after consuming such large prey, but chondros must be able to move through the trees after eating.

Offer hatchlings pinky or fuzzy mice until they are large enough to eat hopper mice. As they continue to grow, you can gradually increase the size of the rodent. Once they are about 3-feet-long, green tree pythons can consume adult mice.

Many keepers continue to feed their adult pythons mice. However, large adults may require more than one mouse per feeding. Large adults are usually big enough to consume small rats.

4) How to Offer Food

Always offer food to your snake when the room is calm and free of pets, rowdy children, and other distractions. Frightened or stressed snakes rarely eat. Additionally, feeding mistakes can be lead to accidental bites.

Some snakes prefer to eat in low light conditions, while others may respond best during the middle of the day. The first step in feeding is to gather thawed, dry rodent and a pair of long forceps, tweezers or tongs. Then, open the cage door or remove the lid and set it aside.

Grab the food item with the forceps. Grip it behind the shoulder blades so that you can produce realistic movements with the item. Place the rodent's nose against a light bulb or in some very hot water for a few minutes to warm it up. Usually, the combination of the rodent odor and a good heat signature on the rodent's head is sufficient to elicit a strike. However, some snakes may be reluctant to eat unless the entire rodent is slightly warm.

Move the food item about 3 or 4 inches in front of the snake's nose. If he is hungry and ready to eat, he may begin flicking his tongue. If so, you can gently place it closer to his face, wiggling it slightly.

Be patient, and allow the snake to gather his nerve and strike the food item. As soon as the snake strikes, try to release the mouse. With a bit of luck, the snake will constrict the rodent as if it were alive. Once this happens, slowly move back and out of the snake's line of sight.

Check on the snake in about five minutes, and be sure that he is still eating the rodent. (Do not leave the area where your snake is with the cage door open. If you can observe it from a distance, leave the door or lid open while backing away. If this will not be possible, try to close the cage as slowly as possible to prevent spooking the snake).

Some snakes are prone to "forgetting" their dinner after they constrict it for a moment. This is usually not a big problem, as most snakes will accept the same rodent if re-offered. Some keepers have found that if you twitch the rodent slightly once the python has constricted it (to simulate the struggles of the rodent) it may help keep the snake focused on the job.

If your snake does not begin tongue flicking when presented with the rodent, try to animate the rodent's movements a little. Wiggle it from left to right quickly and try to elicit tongue flicks.

Investigatory tongue flicks are different from causal, exploratory flicks. They are much more rapid, deliberate and the tongue often remains extended for a prolonged period of time.

If your movements do not generate any interest in the snake, gently move the rodent until it contacts the snake's nose gently. If successful, this may finally get the snake's attention, but often it will cause the snake to hide his head. If this happens, discard the rodent, replace the cage lid and try again in a day or two.

Do not despair if your snake does not eat the first time you offer food. Many times, the snake may still be adjusting to his new home. Alternatively, he could be entering a shed cycle, during which time most snakes refuse food.

If your snake fails to eat after three different attempts, wait one full week before trying again. This should be enough time to allow him to shed or make it obvious that he is about to do so (opaque eyes, milky look to the skin).

5) Problem Feeders

It is not always possible to get a baby snake to begin accepting food voluntarily – this is when purchasing a snake from a reputable breeder pays off. Few breeders will sell their snakes before they are accepting food regularly and eagerly. If repeated attempts fail to yield positive results, you must take steps to jumpstart the process.

Once the snake refuses food for the fourth time (with at least one week elapsing to ensure shedding cycles are not the problem) contact the breeder, if you have not done so already.

Often, the breeder will be able to offer you tips or suggestions that may bring success. If you purchased the snake from a retail establishment, you can request suggestions, but substantial help is not as likely to follow.

6) Feeding Frequency

Most green tree pythons will thrive on a diet of one suitably sized rodent per week. This much food may even cause some adults to gain weight. In general, most captive snakes are fed far more than they would eat in the wild.

Most snakes consume between two and four times their body mass per year (Rossi, 2006). Therefore, if you intend to feed your 1-pound snake once per week, each meal should be roughly 0.05 to .1 pounds, which is approximately the weight of a large adult mouse.

7) Safety at Feeding Time

Many green tree python bites result from feeding mistakes. It is always important to pay attention to your movements and actions when feeding snakes, and be sure that you use tongs that are long enough to keep you out of your snake's strike range.

Never reach into your snake's cage while your hands smell like mice, rats, birds, lizards or other potential prey. Additionally, be aware that snakes are often very aggressive eaters after they have already eaten one prey item – be especially careful at this time.

8) Avoiding Regurgitation

If a snake is stressed or exposed to inappropriate temperatures, it may vomit any recently eaten food items. In addition to being a very unpleasant mess to clean up and a waste of money, vomiting is hard on the snake's body.

To avoid vomiting, always ensure your snake's habitat is the proper temperature, especially after eating. Additionally, refrain from handling your snake as long as a visible lump is present in his body. Even if the food item is too small to make a noticeable lump, refrain from handling a snake for at least 24 hours after feeding them.

If your snake vomits a food item, clean the cage immediately. Additionally, ensure that your snake can rehydrate properly. Many experienced keepers make it a practice to soak snakes after vomiting to ensure hydration.

Give snakes that vomit at least one full week before offering food again. One of the biggest mistakes keepers make when dealing with a snake that has regurgitated is that they try to make up for the lost meal too quickly. This is hard on the snake's digestive system and often causes long-term, chronic problems.

Chapter 8: Green Tree Python Hydration

Like most other animals, green tree pythons require drinking water to remain healthy. However, the amount of water in the air (humidity) is an important factor in their health as well.

1) Drinking Water

Contrary to popular perception, green tree pythons readily drink from water bowls. Provide your pet with access to clean, fresh water at all times.

While it is acceptable to offer the snakes a bowl that will accommodate the snake, it is not necessary. Many keepers use bowls with 4- to 6-inch diameters. Be sure to avoid filling large containers too high, as they are apt to overflow if the snake crawls into the bowl.

Green tree pythons are muscular creatures that may tip their water bowl, so use a bowl heavy or wide enough that the snake will not tip it inadvertently. Plastic trays, such as clean cat litter pans, also work very well for supplying your snake with water.

Be sure to check the water dish daily and ensure that the water is clean. Empty, wash and refill the water dish any time it is contaminated with substrate, shed skin, urates or feces.

Some keepers prefer to use dechlorinated or bottled water for their snakes; however, untreated tap water is used by many keepers with no ill effects.

2) Humidity

Green tree pythons come from very humid habitats, and they require moderate humidity levels in captivity.

As a rule of thumb, green tree pythons are comfortable at humidity levels of about 60 to 70 percent, although they will tolerate much higher humidity levels, as long as the cage is not wet.

While experienced keepers are often successful maintaining suitable humidity levels without precise measurements, beginners should monitor the humidity. Beginning snake keepers should consider acquiring and utilizing a hygrometer in their snake's cage to measure the relative humidity level. Be aware though, economy "stick-on" hygrometers seldom yield accurate results. Many digital thermometers are capable of measuring relative humidity in addition to temperature.

Humidity levels vary greatly from one snake keeper's residence to another; different keepers will need to use different strategies for maintaining suitable humidity levels. There are several different ways to increase the humidity of your pet's habitat, so experiment with different strategies to arrive at the best solution for your situation.

There are two primary ways of increasing the relative humidity: Add more water to the cage, or restrict the amount of water that is allowed to evaporate from the cage.

Adding Water
Most keepers will achieve suitable humidity levels by simply incorporating a large water dish into the habitat. The volume of water is not as important as the surface area of the water. In other words, a shallow, wide dish will raise the cage humidity more than a narrow, deeper water bowl will.

Placing the water dish under a heat lamp or over a heating pad will help accelerate the evaporation rate, but it will require you to refill the water dish more frequently.

You can also dampen the substrate to elevate the humidity level inside the cage. The damp (not wet) substrate will slowly release the water into the air in the cage, thus elevating the humidity. This works best with moisture-retaining substrates, such as cypress mulch or orchid bark. However, you can also dampen newspaper and similar substrates.

Misting

Another way to raise the humidity in the cage is by misting the substrate and interior surfaces of the enclosure with lukewarm water.

It is perfectly safe to spray your snake (gently) with clean, lukewarm water, but be aware that some snakes do not like to be sprayed. Green tree pythons may twitch or hiss when you first spray them, but they usually begin drinking or simply hide their heads. Avoid spraying a snake in the face – this often results in a defensive strike.

Snake that react badly to misting may be more comfortable when "rained" on, rather than misted. You can accomplish this by misting the ceiling of the cage. The water will tend to collect on the surface, and fall down onto the snake in large drops.

Keepers with one snake will usually find a simple, handheld spray bottle to be sufficient. Keepers with many snakes are better served by acquiring a compressed-air sprayer.

Always allow the standing water droplets to evaporate or soak into the substrate between mistings – the cage should not stay wet for extended periods of time.

In addition to increasing the cage humidity temporarily, misting often causes green tree pythons to become active. This benefits them by encouraging exercise, mental stimulation, and, often, it causes them to defecate. Misting is also a stimulus used to elicit mating behavior.

One drawback to misting cages is that the water droplets can leave unsightly spots on glass surfaces. Water with a low-mineral content may help eliminate this possibility.

Restricting Airflow

Cages with excess ventilation, such as many aquaria, may allow too much water to evaporate from the cage. To prevent this from happening, you can attach a piece of glass or plastic to a portion of the screened areas of the cage. This will reduce the amount of water that evaporates from the cage. You do not want to reduce the ventilation too much, so only cover as much of the cage as is necessary to raise the humidity.

If you use an air conditioner in your home during the summer or the heater during the winter, you may find that your cages dry out faster than normal. Both such units reduce the humidity of the air in your home, which will tend to draw moisture out of the cage.

Live Plants
Live plants are an excellent tool for raising the humidity in a cage. Plants engage in a process known as transpiration, in which they draw water from the ground and release it via small openings in the plant leaves. Additionally, live plants can serve as "canaries in cold mines."

If your plant starts to wilt, it does not have enough water. It also means that humidity level in the cage is probably substandard. By taking care of the plant – which will succumb to dehydration faster than the snake will – the keeper is essentially assured of maintaining proper humidity levels.

Live plants also provide cover for the snake, which is especially helpful when raising young snakes. The surface of the leaves will also collect water when the cage is misted, which also raises the humidity level.

Many different plants are suitable for use in your green tree python's cage. Some of the most popular plants used by keepers include pothos, bromeliads and ficus trees, but virtually any non-toxic species that will tolerate low light levels and frequent watering will work.

Some common cage plants -- notably golden pothos plants (*Epipremnum aureum*) – will survive when planted in water; they do not need soil to survive.

3) Soaking Snakes

In addition to providing drinking water, many keepers soak their green tree pythons periodically in a tub of clean, lukewarm water. Soaking is helpful tool for the husbandry of many snakes, including chondros, who hail from very humid habitats.

In addition to ensuring that your snake remains adequately hydrated, soaks help to remove dirt and encourage complete, problem-free sheds. It is not necessary to soak your snake if it remains adequately hydrated, but most green tree pythons benefit from an occasional soak.

Soaks should last a maximum of about one hour, and be performed no more often than once per week (unless the snake is experiencing shedding difficulties).

When soaking your snake, the water should not be very deep. Never make your snake swim to keep its head above water. Ideally, snakes should be soaked in containers with only enough water to cover their back. This should allow your snake to rest comfortably with its head above water.

Never leave a snake unattended while it is soaking.

If your snake defecates in the water, be sure to rinse him off with clean water before returning him to his cage.

Chapter 9: Interacting with Green tree pythons

1) Handling

One of the most enjoyable aspects of snake keeping for many people is handling their pet. However, green tree pythons should not be handled excessively, which can cause them considerable stress.

While many chondros learn to accept regular, gentle interaction, others may never settle down enough for regular handling. Nevertheless, learning the proper techniques will increase the chances that the snake will become docile over time. This will make handling time more enjoyable for you and less stressful for your pet.

Do not handle young green tree pythons, who are less than 1 year old. The tiny snakes are simply too delicate for inexperienced human hands, and it is very easy to cause permanent damage to them. You must still be very gentle when handling yearlings, and it is preferable to restrict handling to mature animals.

Picking Up the Perch
The easiest way to manipulate your green tree python is by simply removing the perch that he is resting on.

If your snake is tame, you can simply remove the perch and hold it in your hands. You can now inspect your snake closely, or try to encourage him to crawl off the perch and into your hands.

The best way to begin is by gently lifting his head, which may spur him to explore his surroundings. As he slowly releases his grip on the perch, allow it to fall away, but keep holding the snake. Do not try to pull the snake off his perch, as it may damage his vertebrae or tail. Always be sure to support the weight of the snake and the perch completely.

If your snake is aggressive, it may help to drape a few large pieces of newspaper or fabric over him. This will usually cause even the most aggressive snakes to sit relatively calmly. You can then grip the perch and remove it from the cage.

Removing the Snake from Its Perch

It is not easy to remove a green tree python from its perch. Nevertheless, it is occasionally necessary, so you must know how to do it.

Whenever possible, try to encourage your snake to crawl off his perch voluntarily. This takes a great deal of patience, as green tree pythons tend to move slowly and deliberately.

If you must remove the snake from his perch (for veterinary care, etc.) and he will not do so voluntarily, you will have to employ another strategy.

The key to removing green tree pythons from their perches is doing so quickly, gently and deliberately.

1. Open the cage door.
2. Immediately place both of your hands over the snake. Keep your palms together and fingers pointing in opposite directions.
3. Gently slide each hand's fingertips under the snake's coils. Be sure that you feel for the delicate tail, and hold it gently – but securely – in your hand so that it cannot grip the perch.
4. Gently "open" the snake by bending each hand back at the same time.
5. With the snake now securely in each hand, remove the snake from the cage.

Do not stand in front of the cage for extended periods of time, trying to gather the nerve to pick up your snake. This often makes snakes nervous. The goal is for your snake to learn to anticipate the activity and react calmly.

It is important to consider that some snakes may never become tractable, trustworthy pets. You will still need to care for your snake if this happens, and you need to have a plan of action for doings so.

Baby green tree pythons must be handled as little as possible. When it is necessary to hold them, you must use a very light touch to avoid hurting them.

Holding the Snake

When holding a snake, avoid restraining it. Instead, seek to support its body weight, and allow it to crawl from one hand to the other. It is always wise to handle the snake over a table or other object to prevent his from falling to the floor, should he make a sudden move.

Usually, your green tree python will grip your hands or arm quite securely, as though you were a tree. This can cause new keepers a bit of apprehension, but with time, you will become used to it.

Always realize that you are responsible for your snake while you are holding it. Accidents can and have happened. Such occurrences are very bad for snakes, snake keepers and the entire snake-keeping hobby, and must be avoided. Never handle your snake in a public situation.

Do not take your snake to the park or to the local fast food restaurant. Your snake is not a toy, he does not appreciate "hanging out" in this manner, and it makes snake keepers everywhere look bad.

Snakes frighten many people and you should always be sensitive to this fact. Rather than playing into these fears, seek to educate people about snakes rather than shock them by bringing them to inappropriate events and locations.

Safely Handling Green Tree Pythons
Even when completely tame, green tree pythons must be handled with respect. Avoid placing the snake near your face (or anyone else's face).

Always be sure to avoid smelling like potential prey when handling green tree pythons. While a defensive bite can cause damage, a feeding-response bite is much more likely to cause serious injury.

Do not handle chondros in the presence of unsupervised children or pets.

Additionally, as green tree pythons may be more aggressive and active during low-light conditions, it is safer to handle them during the day, with the lights on.

2) In The Event of a Bite

If your chondros bites you, remain calm. Most defensive bites involve a quick strike-bite-release, whereas feeding mistakes usually cause the green tree python to hold on and potentially begin constricting.

If it is a defensive bite, and the snake releases its hold, close the cage or return the snake to his enclosure. Then, wash the wound thoroughly with soap and warm water. Consult your doctor if the bite is serious, will not stop bleeding or you can feel teeth lodged in the wound.

If the snake does not release his grip, the best thing to do is place him in a bucket of cold water. Alternatively, you can hold him under cold, running water.

Wash the wound, and contact your doctor.

3) Temporary Transport Cages

The best way to transport your snake is with a plastic storage container. The container must have ample air holes to allow ventilation and it must be safe and secure.

Some keepers prefer transparent boxes for such purposes, as they allow you to see the snake while it is inside the box. This is definitely a benefit – especially when opening and closing the box – but opaque transportation boxes provide your snake with more security, as they cannot see the activity going on outside their container.

Place a few paper towels or some clean newspaper in the bottom of the box to give your snake somewhere to hide and to absorb any fluids, should your snake defecate or discharge urates.

While not imperative, some keepers like to include a perch for their snake in transportation boxes. This will undoubtedly make your snake more secure during outings.

If possible, consider using transportation cages that will accommodate the same perches that are in the snake's cage. This way, you can simply remove the snake and his perch, place the perch in the transportation container and be on your way.

4) Transporting Tips

When traveling with your snake, pay special attention to the temperature. Use the air-conditioning or heater in your vehicle to keep the snake within his comfortable range (the mid-70s Fahrenheit are ideal in most circumstances).

Do not jostle your snake unnecessarily, nor leave it unattended in a car. Make sure that the transport container is secure – in the unfortunate circumstance in which you are in an accident, a loose snake is not an additional problem with which you need to contend.

Do not take your snake with you on public transportation.

5) Hygiene

Always practice good hygiene when handling snakes. Wash your hands with soap and warm water each time you touch your snake, his habitat or the tools you use to care for him.

Never wash cages or tools in kitchens or bathrooms that are used by humans.

Chapter 10: Common Health Concerns

Unlike humans, who can tell you when they are sick, snakes endure illness stoically. This does not mean that injury or illnesses do not cause them distress, but without expressive facial features, they do not look like they are suffering.

In fact, many snake illnesses do not produce symptoms until the disease has already reached an advanced state. Accordingly, it is important to treat injuries and illness promptly to provide your pet with the best chance of recovery.

Acquiring competent veterinary care for a tropical snake is not as easy as finding a veterinarian to treat a dog or cat. Those living in major metropolitan areas are likely to find one reasonably close, but rural snake keepers may have to take great lengths to find a suitable vet.

1) Finding a Suitable Veterinarian

Relatively few veterinarians treat snakes and other reptiles. It is important to find a snake-oriented veterinarian before you need one. There are a number of ways to do this:

- You can search veterinarian databases to find one that is local and treats reptiles.
- You can inquire with your dog or cat veterinarian to see if he or she knows a qualified reptile-oriented veterinarian to whom he or she can refer you.
- You can contact a local reptile-enthusiast group or club. Most such organizations will be familiar with the local veterinarians.
- You can inquire with local nature preserves or zoos. Most such institutions have relationships with veterinarians that treat reptiles and other exotic animals.

If you happen to live in a remote area and do not have a reptile-oriented veterinarian within driving distance, you can try to find a conventional veterinarian who will treat your animal after consulting with a reptile-oriented veterinarian. Such visits may be expensive, as you will have to pay for two veterinary visits (the actual visit and the phone consultation), but it may be your only choice.

2) Reasons to Visit the Veterinarian

While snakes do not require vaccinations or similar routine treatments, they may require visits for other reasons. Anytime your snake exhibits signs of illness or suffers an injury, you must visit the veterinarian.

Visit your veterinarian when:

- You first acquire your snake. This will allow your veterinarian to familiarize himself or herself with your pet while it is presumably healthy. This gives him or her a baseline against which he or she can consider future deviations. Additionally, your veterinarian may be able to diagnose existing illnesses, before they cause serious problems.
- The time your snake wheezes, exhibits labored breathing or produces a mucus discharge from its nostrils or mouth.
- Your snake produces soft or watery feces. (Soft feces are expected when snakes are fed some food items, such as birds. This is not necessarily cause for concern.)
- Your snake suffers any significant injury. Common examples include thermal burns, friction damage to the rostral (nose) region or damaged scales.
- Reproductive issues occur, such as being unable to deliver young. If a snake appears nervous, agitated or otherwise stressed and unable to give birth, see your veterinarian immediately.
- Your snake fails to feed for an extended period. While many snakes fast from time to time – which is no cause

for concern – a veterinarian should see any new snake that does not eat for 4 weeks. Snakes that have been in your care, and normally eat aggressively, may fast for longer than this without ill effects.

3) Common Health Problems

Some of the common health problems, their causes and suggested course of action follow.

This green tree python has retained a significant portion of his shed skin. The skin has peeled off his face and head, but large portions remain on his back and sides.

Retained or Poor Sheds

Captive snakes – especially in the hands of novice keepers – often shed poorly. Due to their exceptionally thin skin and need for high humidity, this problem is especially common with green tree pythons.

With proper husbandry, healthy snakes should produce one-piece sheds regularly (if the shed skin is broken in one or two places, but comes off easily, there is no cause for concern).

Retained sheds can cause health problems, particularly if they restrict blood flow. This is often a problem when a snake retains a bit of old skin near the tail tip.

If your snake sheds poorly, you must take steps to remove the old skin and review your husbandry to prevent the problem from happening again. If you are providing ideal husbandry parameters, and yet your snake still experiences poor sheds, consult your veterinarian to rule out illness.

The best way to remove retained sheds is by soaking your snake or placing him in a damp container for about an hour. After removing him, see if you can gently peel the skin off. Try to keep the skin in as few pieces as possible to make the job easier.

Do not force the skin off your snake. If it does not come off easily, return him to his cage and repeat the process again in 12 to 24 hours. Usually, repeated soaks or time in a damp hide will loosen the skin sufficiently to be removed.

If repeated treatments do not yield results, consult your veterinarian. He may feel that the retained shed is not causing a problem, and advise you to leave it attached – it should come off with the snake's next shed. Alternatively, it if is causing a problem, the veterinarian can remove it without much risk of harming your snake.

Retained Spectacles

Unlike a simple retained shed, a retained spectacle (eye cap) is a serious matter. Do not try to remove a retained spectacle yourself; simply keep the snake in a humid environment and take it to your veterinarian, who should be able to remove it relatively easily.

Respiratory Infections

Like humans, snakes can suffer from respiratory infections. Snakes with respiratory infections exhibit fluid or mucus draining from their nose and/or mouth, may be lethargic and are unlikely to eat. They may also spend excessive amounts of time basking on or under the heat source, in an effort to induce a "behavioral fever."

Bacteria, or, less frequently, fungi or parasites often cause respiratory infections. In addition, cleaning products, perfumes, pet dander and other particulate matter can irritate a snake's respiratory tract as well. Some such bacteria are ubiquitous, and only become problematic when they overwhelm a snake's immune system. Other bacteria (and most viruses) are transmitted from one snake to another.

To reduce the chances of illnesses, keep your snake quarantined from other snakes, keep his enclosure exceptionally clean and be sure to provide the best husbandry possible, in terms of temperature and humidity. Additionally, avoid stressing your snake by handling him too frequently, or exposing him to chaotic situations.

Upon taking your snake to the vet, he or she will likely take samples of the mucus and have it analyzed to determine the causal agent. The veterinarian will then prescribe medications, if appropriate, such as antibiotics.

It is imperative to carry out the actions prescribed by your veterinarian exactly as stated, and keep your snake's stress level very low while he is healing. Stress can reduce immune function, so avoid handling him unnecessarily, and consider covering the front of his cage while he recovers.

Many snakes produce audible breathing sounds for a few days immediately preceding a shed cycle. This is rarely cause for concern and will resolve once the snake sheds. However, if you are in doubt, always seek veterinary attention.

"Mouth Rot"
Mouth rot – properly called stomatitis – is identified by noting discoloration, discharge or cheesy-looking material in the snake's mouth. Mouth rot can be a serious illness, and requires the attention of your veterinarian.

While mouth rot can follow an injury (such as happens when a snake strikes the side of a glass cage) it can also arise from systemic illness. Your veterinarian will cleanse your snake's mouth and potentially prescribe an antibiotic.

Your veterinarian may recommend withholding food until the problem is remedied. Always be sure that snakes recovering from mouth rot have immaculately clean habitats, with ideal temperatures.

Internal Parasites

In the wild, most snakes carry some internal parasites. While it may not be possible to keep a snake completely free of internal parasites, it is important to keep these levels in check.

Consider any wild-caught snake to be parasitized until proven otherwise. While most captive bred snakes should have relatively few internal parasites, they can suffer from such problems as well.

Preventing parasites from building to pathogenic levels requires strict hygiene. Many parasites build up to dangerous levels when the snakes are kept in a cage that is continuously contaminated from feces.

Most internal parasites that are of importance for snakes are transmitted via the fecal-oral route. This means that eggs (or a similar life stage) of the parasites are released with the feces. If the snake inadvertently ingests these, the parasites can develop inside the snake's body and cause increased problems. Such eggs are usually microscopic and easily lifted into the air, where they may stick to cage walls or land in the water dish. Later, when the snake flicks its tongue or drinks from the water dish, it ingests the eggs.

Internal parasites may cause your snake to vomit, pass loose stools, and fail to grow or refuse food entirely. Other parasites may produce no symptoms at all, demonstrating the importance of routine examinations.

Your veterinarian will usually examine your snake's feces if he suspects internal parasites. By looking at the type of eggs inside the snake's feces, you veterinarian can prescribe an appropriate medication. Many parasites are easily treated with anti-parasitic medications, but often, these medications must be given several times to eradicate the pathogens completely.

Some parasites may be transmissible to people, so always take proper precautions, including regular hand washing and keeping snakes and their cages away from kitchens and other areas where foods are prepared.

Examples of common internal parasites include roundworms, tapeworms and amoebas.

External Parasites
The primary external parasites that afflict snakes are ticks and snake mites. Ticks are rare on captive bred animals, but wild caught snakes often have a few.

Ticks should be removed manually. Using tweezers grasp the tick as close as possible to the snake's skin and pull with steady, gentle pressure. Do not place anything over the tick first, such as petroleum jelly, or carry out any other "home remedies," such as burning the tick with a match. Such techniques may cause the tick to inject more saliva (which may contain diseases or bacteria) into the snake's body.

Drop the tick in a jar of isopropyl alcohol to ensure it is killed. It is a good idea to bring these to your veterinarian for analysis. Do not contact ticks with your bare hands, as many species can transmit disease to humans.

Mites are another matter entirely. While ticks are generally large enough to see easily, mites are about the size of a pepper flake. Whereas tick infestations usually only tally a few individuals, mite infestations may include thousands of individual parasites.

Mites may afflict wild caught snakes, but, as they are not confined to a small cage, such infestations are somewhat self-limiting. However, in captivity, mite infestations can approach plague proportions.

After a female mite feeds on a snake, she drops off and finds a safe place (such as a tiny crack in a cage or among the substrate) to deposit her eggs. After the eggs hatch, they travel back to your snake (or to other snakes in your collection) where they feed and perpetuate the lifecycle.

Whereas a few mites may represent little more than an inconvenience to the snake, a significant infection stresses them considerably, and may even cause death through anemia. This is particularly true for small or young animals. Additionally, mites may transmit disease from one snake to another.

There are a number of different methods for eradicating a mite infestation. In each case, there are two primary steps that must be taken: You must eradicate the snake's parasites, and eradicate the parasites in the snake's environment (which includes the room in which the cage resides).

It is relatively simple to remove mites from a snake. When mites get wet, they die. However, mites are protected by a thick, waxy exoskeleton that encourages the formation of an air bubble. This means that you cannot place your snake in water to drown the mites. The mites will simply hide under the snake's scales, using their air bubble to protect themselves.

To defeat this waxy cuticle, all that is needed is a few drops of gentle dish soap added to the water. The soap will lower the surface tension of water, allowing it to penetrate under the snake's scales. Additionally, the soap disrupts the surface tension of the water, preventing the air bubble from forming.

By soaking your snake is the slightly soapy water for about one hour will kill most of the mites on his body. Use care when doing so, but try to arrange the water level and container so that most of the snake's body is below the water.

While the snake is soaking, perform a thorough cage cleaning. Remove everything from the cage, including water dishes, substrates and cage props. Sterilize all impermeable cage items, and discard the substrate and all porous cage props. Vacuum the area around the cage and wipe down all of the nearby surfaces with a wet cloth.

It may be necessary to repeat this process several times to eradicate the mites completely. Accordingly, the very best strategy is to avoid contracting mites in the first place. This is why it is important to purchase your snake from a reliable breeder or retailer, and keep your snake quarantined from potential mite vectors.

As an example, even if you purchase your snake from a reliable source, provide excellent husbandry and clean the cage regularly, you can end up battling mites if your friend brings his snake – which has a few mites – to your house.

It may be possible for mites to crawl onto your hands or clothes, hop off when you return home and make their way to your snake. This is why many breeders and experienced hobbyists avoid visiting low-quality pet stores or places with poorly tended snake cages.

While it is relatively easy to observe mites on a snake that has a significant infestation, a few mites may go unnoticed. Make it a practice to inspect your snake and his cage regularly. Look in the crease under the snake's lower jaw, near the eyes and near the vent; all of these are places in which mites hide. It can also be helpful to wipe down your snake with a damp, white paper towel. After wiping down the snake, observe the towel to see if any mites are present.

Chemical treatments are also available to combat mites, but you must be very careful with such substances. Beginners should rely on their veterinarian to prescribe or suggest the appropriate chemicals.

Avoid repurposing lice treatments or other chemicals, as is often encouraged by other hobbyists. Such non-intended use may be very dangerous, and it is often in violation of Federal laws.

New hobbyists should consult with their veterinarian if they suspect that their snake has mites. Mite eradication is often a challenging ordeal that your veterinarian can help make easier.

Long-Term Anorexia

While short-term fasts of one to two weeks are common among snakes, fasts that last longer than this may be cause for concern. If your snake refuses food, ensure that its habitat is set up ideally with ample hiding opportunities and access to appropriate temperatures.

If none of these factors are inappropriate, and therefore likely to be causing the problem, consult your veterinarian. Above all, do not panic – snakes can go very long periods of time without food. Your veterinarian will want to make sure that your snake is in good health, as respiratory infections or internal parasites may cause it to refuse food.

Some snakes refuse food in the winter or breeding season, as would happen in the wild. While you should consult with your veterinarian the first time this happens, subsequent refusals during such times do not usually indicate a problem.

Mouth rot, respiratory illness and parasites can cause snakes to refuse food.

Chapter 11: Geographic Locales and Selectively Bred Lines

Part of the appeal of chondros is the variety of colors that different individuals display. Many wild green tree pythons are clad in numerous white dots atop an emerald green base color, while others display sky-blue dorsal stripes that contrast with their grassy green body color. Still others develop a dusting of black or retain significant portions of their juvenile yellow color.

In captivity, breeders have produced animals that resemble these naturally occurring snakes, as well as animals that have no business bearing the name "green" tree python. Many breeders seek to produce uniformly yellow or blue snakes – in many cases they have succeeded.

The variation present in the species is truly amazing.

Nevertheless, within this natural variation, relatively few single-gene mutations have been found. While ball python (Python regius) breeders may have access to genetic mutations, such as amelanism, anerythrism, hypomelanism, hypermelanism and many others, the only single-gene mutation known in green tree pythons is the amelanistic mutation.

Generally speaking, the different appearances of green tree pythons precipitate from the interactions of many different genes. This makes it more difficult to predict the outcome of breeding projects.

Nevertheless, it still behooves prospective chondro owners to learn about the ways in which mutations are often inherited.

1) Patterns of Inheritance

Different traits are inherited in different ways.

Snakes receive one copy of each gene from their mother and one from their father. Some genes affect the animal's appearance when only one copy is present, while others require two copies of a gene to express the associated trait.

When an animal has two copies of the same gene, it is said to be homozygous. When an animal has one copy of a mutant gene and one copy of the normal gene, it is called heterozygous.

Simple Recessive
Simple recessive traits are only expressed when an animal has two copies of the mutant gene. However, normal looking, but heterozygous animals may produce offspring that display the trait associated with the gene, if the other parent has a copy of the gene as well.

Currently, the amelanistic/albino gene is the only known simple recessive trait in green tree pythons. However, some workers hypothesize that the yellow hatchling color is a recessive trait as well.

Dominant

Dominant traits are expressed whenever they are present, regardless of the other gene in the pair. Accordingly, dominant traits become very common in a given gene pool. The natural "wild" appearance of pythons is usually dominant over most genes, although there are exceptions.

There is no visual difference between an animal with one copy of the gene or two copies of the gene. However, a dominant animal that is homozygous for the mutation only produces young that display the morph.

Incompletely Dominant
Incompletely dominant mutations are similar to dominant mutations except that those with one copy of the gene look different from those with two copies of the mutant gene do.

Often, homozygous animals have a more extreme version of the color or pattern mutation, than heterozygous animals do.

Often, incompletely dominant mutations are called co-dominant mutations. However, this terminology is not technically correct. Animals that display co-dominant traits exhibit a combination of two or more genes.

Polygenetic Traits

Groups of genes influence most green tree python traits, like pattern and ground color. A human example of a polygenetic trait is adult height, which is determined by myriad genes that interact with each other. Accordingly, full siblings can have vastly different heights.

Most aspects of green tree python color and pattern appear to be polygenetic. For example, consider blue dorsal striping, which occurs in some, but not all, green tree pythons.

If you were to breed two pythons with bold blue stripes together, the resulting clutch will likely display young snakes with a range of blue stripes. Some will have even bolder stripes than their parents do, while some may lack a stripe entirely. The majority of the clutch will fall somewhere between these two extremes.

Over time, these traits can be emphasized through selective breeding efforts. These types of projects have resulted in green tree pythons that are described as high blue, high yellow, quad-colored, mite-phase or any number of other names.

2) Geographic Forms

Found all over the island of New Guinea, several offshore island groups and northern Australia, green tree pythons exhibit significant variation in their colors, patterns and morphologies.

While each area produces a wide range of appearances, some visual traits are common in animals originating from some areas. However, short of traveling to New Guinea and catching your own green tree python, it is impossible to be certain where your snake originated.

In addition to simple complications, such as mistaken paperwork, some green tree pythons are labelled as being from a particular geographic region as a way to inflate their prices. Usually, locality specific forms are more expensive than those whose origin is unknown.

Additionally, these snakes are often labelled as originating from the area in which the exporter's facility (or the airport) resides. For instance, many green tree pythons are labelled as originating from Jayapura. However, Jayapura is a city that has few – if any green tree pythons – within its general range. Jayapura happens to be the location that many green tree pythons are routed through, as they make their way to the United States and Europe – but the snakes may have been collected in some other area.

Given the individual variation found among snakes from the same geographic area and the lack of accurate information regarding wild caught green tree pythons who are sold into the pet trade, it is difficult to know where a given snake originated.

This has led many green tree pythons to label their snakes as "types," rather than definitively coming from a given area. For example, keepers will call a snake that looks like the green tree pythons from Aru, an "Aru type." The only time the "type" designation is dropped is when the snakes have sufficient documentation and provenance to ensure that they actually were collected (or hail from parents collected) in a given region.

While it is important to understand that variation exists, the following descriptions fairly characterize the snakes coming from different locations. Understand that not every location produces unique looking animal; Yapen and Biak, for example, are two different island groups, whose animals are virtually identical.

Aru, Merauke and Australian animals belong to the southern lineage of green tree python. Green tree pythons from all other locations are members of the northern lineage. Currently, all chondros are classified as the same species, and no subspecies are recognized.

Aru

"Aru type" green tree pythons are among the most popular geographic forms available. The Aru Islands are a small group of islands off the southwest coast of New Guinea. The first green tree python documented by scientists (called the holotype) was caught on one of these islands.

They are characterized by deep, emerald green coloration, white ventral surfaces and scattered white and blue flecks. Many develop extensive blue washes over their ventral and lateral surfaces.

Aru types are almost always yellow when they hatch and they have blunt tail-tips throughout their lives. Many Aru types are docile and easy to handle. Aru types grow quite large, and are likely the second largest population of green tree pythons.

Merauke

Merauke is a mainland locale, located in the southern portion of New Guinea. Merauke animals are usually bright green. Some wild caught animals have white dorsal stripes, but others possess only scattered yellow and white scales.

Some authorities suspect that animals that are labelled as "Merauke" or "Merauke types," are actually from farther inland. Merauke is situated along the southern boundary of New Guinea, in a habitat that is unlikely to hold many green tree pythons. Instead, Merauke is likely an exit point from which many southern green tree pythons are exported from the country. Most of the snakes labelled as such probably originate from Tanah Merah and other locations.

The first albino chondro was produced from Merauke type ancestors. Meraukes often undergo rather sudden color changes.

Australia

Australian animals are not available in the United States or Europe. However, they resemble Merauke-locale animals in most respects. Australian animals are predominately green, but some have subtle blue markings or scattered yellow or white scales.

Red babies have never been observed from any Australian green tree python.

Sorong

Sorong type animals tend to have blue dorsal stripes, deep green coloration and yellow ventral surfaces. The hatchlings are usually yellow. Sorong types are some of the smallest green tree pythons, and they have very beautiful heads with prominent lobes. Sorong types often have long, black tails.

Manokwari

Manokwari type animals are famous for possessing very striking blue markings along their backs. They resemble Sorong-type individuals, and have a similar, deep green ground color. However, the dorsal stripping of Manokwari types is usually broken at several places.

Most Manokwari babies are yellow. Like Sorong types (who also hail from the same general region – the Bird's Head Peninsula), Manokwari types tend to be small, elegant-looking snakes.

Wamena

Wamena is a highland location, found on the northern side of the central mountain range. Most of the animals from this region have dark green coloration. Young Wamena types may be red or yellow. Some animals develop black speckling during the color change process. Occasionally, these markings are retained into adulthood. Wamena types usually have a complete, but rather indistinct, blue dorsal stripe.

Just like Merauke types, most Wamena types probably originate in other areas, but they are exported from Wamena.

Cyclops Mountains

Cyclops animals typically look like other highland animals with one noteworthy distinction – they usually have white clusters of scales (often called rosettes) along their blue dorsal stripes. Cyclops animals are somewhat rare in captive collections.

Biak

Biak animals are among the most variable and distinctive of the locality types. Hatchlings may be either red or yellow, and the color change process usually occurs over many years. Biak types are often irritable snakes, but they have some of the best food drives of any geographic location.

Biak types likely grow larger than any of the other green tree python populations do. They may display yellow, white, blue, black and gray colors, but their ground color is usually olive green or pale green. Biak type animals have long, "dragon-like" heads and often bear yellow blotches across their faces.

Kofiau

The Kofiau Islands are a small group of islands, located off the east coast of the Bird's Head Peninsula. Kofiau snakes began appearing in the marketplace in the early 2000s. They appear somewhat similar to Sorong types, with one fantastic exception – some of the individuals appear to exhibit extremely delayed color changes, or forgo them entirely.

Much remains to be learned about the snakes from this location. Unfortunately, it appears that collectors may have completely eradicated green tree pythons from these islands. There are a handful of these unique pythons in captivity, but captive reproduction has been limited.

This Biak-type animal demonstrates the characteristic yellow facemask that is common in these snakes.

3) Designer Forms

Some green tree python breeders strive to produce animals that look like wild green tree pythons. Many even pair animals from the same geographic location. However, other breeders desire to produce baby green tree pythons that look like anything but their wild-living cousins.

There is nothing inherently right or wrong about this practice – captive green tree pythons need not worry about camouflage to escape the notice of predators. It is simply a different pursuit.

Such "designer" snakes are often produced by combining different locality types. Each generation, the young with the most appealing aesthetics are retained and bred to other attractive animals to ensure that the next generation looks even more amazing.

Because the aesthetics of these snakes are produced by a variety of genes, the results can be difficult to predict. Sometimes, "average looking" snakes produce incredible offspring, while some of the finest animals in the world still produce the occasional "dud."

For buyers, who usually purchase such animals as hatchlings, a level of risk is involved. The red or yellow hatchling in your hand may become an average adult (for which you paid an exorbitant sum) or it may become one of the best-looking snakes ever produced. You simply cannot tell from the hatchling.

While breeders of designer green tree pythons are continually trying new pairings and developing new goals, some of the most common designer types are described below.

High Yellow

High yellow animals have long been popular among green tree python keepers. Breeders have produced several different high

113

yellow lines and each has different characteristics and attributes. The definition for "high yellow" is not clear-cut – some may use the term for snakes with 10 percent of their bodies covered in yellow, while others may only use the term to refer to mostly yellow animals.

High Blue

Perhaps the most sought-after designer type, blue chondros are very popular among keepers. There are several different types of blue green tree python, with different breeders bestowing different names on the various lines. Most snakes that eventually turn blue were red as babies.

It is important to recognize that many female green tree pythons turn blue after they go through a reproductive cycle. This is usually called "hormonal blue" by hobbyists, and is far more common than genetically blue snakes.

High Black

Sometimes called "mite phase," animals with copious black flecking are often highly sought after. High black lines often originate from highland locations. Many highland locality types develop *temporary* black speckling as they undergo their color change. However, upon maturation, most lose their black colors.

Accordingly, mature animals that display significant black flecking often demand premium prices. Most snakes with significant amounts of black color were red as babies.

Tri- / Quad-Colored

Tri- or quad-colored snakes are usually clad in roughly equal amounts of green, blue and white or green, blue, white and yellow. Often, they trace their roots to high yellow or high blue projects.

All Green

Completely unmarked, all-green individuals are quite rare. A few breeders have attempted to produce all green snakes with varying amounts of success.

Bright / Wide Stripe

Many breeders have worked to emphasize the blue dorsal stripes of some lines, by making the stripes wider or brighter.

Chapter 12: Breeding Green tree pythons

The act of breeding green tree pythons is relatively straightforward. Over the last few decades, breeders have developed a relatively consistent "recipe" for producing captive bred chondros.

1) Pre-Breeding Considerations

Before you set out to breed your green tree pythons, consider the decision carefully. Unfortunately, few keepers realize the implications of breeding their snakes before they set out to do so.

Ask yourself if you will be able to:

- Provide the proper care for the female while gravid
- Afford emergency veterinary services if necessary
- Be willing to remove the eggs from an angry, protective female python's cage.
- Incubate 20 or more eggs in some type of incubator
- Provide housing for 20 or more babies
- Provide food for 20 or more babies
- Dedicate the time to establishing 20 or more babies
- Find the time to care for 20 or more babies
- Find new homes for 20 or more babies
- Afford to heat up to 20 baby snake habitats

Few people are able to do all of these things. While your green tree pythons may not produce 20 eggs or more, it is possible, and you must be prepared to deal with this.

Many people see the price tags associated with many snakes, and instantly envision themselves becoming snake breeders. However, the vast majority of people that try to breed snakes for profit fail.

Becoming a snake breeder means that, depending on the area in which you live, you may have to obtain licenses, insurance or permits to do so legally.

2) Sexing Green tree pythons

Obviously, you must have at least one sexual pair to breed green tree pythons. It is always prudent to verify the gender of snakes, as mistakes are common.

Novices should not attempt to determine the gender of their snakes. Most veterinarians, breeders and pet stores will perform the procedure for a nominal fee.

Sexing Young Green Tree Pythons

Green tree pythons have incredibly delicate tails. If they are handled carelessly, the snakes can develop kinked tails, which will last for the rest of their lives. Accordingly, even the most experienced breeders generally decline requests to determine the gender of young chondros.

In general, green tree pythons should not have their genders determined until they are at least 1 year of age.

Probing

You can determine the gender of green tree pythons by passing a smooth, lubricated steel probe into the cloaca. When moved posteriorly, the probe will penetrate to a much greater depth in males than in females. This occurs because the inserted probe travels down the inside of one of the hidden hemipenes; when inserted into a female, no such space accepts the probe.

"Popping"

Some snake keepers utilize a technique called "popping" to determine the gender of their snakes. Popping involves applying gentle pressure to the base of a snake's tail. When performed on males, this often makes the hemipenes evert; obviously, this does not occur in females.

Popping is an effective method for determining the gender of very young snakes, but by the time snakes have reached a few months of age, they have sufficient muscle strength to resist the pressure applied by the keeper. Popping is simply not effective for determining the gender of mature snakes.

Since young green tree pythons should not be popped, and adults cannot be popped reliably, the technique is not very helpful for green tree pythons.

3) Pre-Breeding Conditioning

Snakes should be well fed, but not obese, before breeding. Some keepers increase the amount of food offered to females prior to cycling, but others feel that the standard diet is sufficient. In most cases, captive snakes eat more food than their wild counterparts do, so typical feeding schedules are adequate.

Maturity is likely related to size more than age; maturity may be obtained in as little as 18 months or as long as 5 years. Males are usually capable of breeding by the time they are about 3 to 3 ½ feet long, although some may breed successfully before reaching this size.

Females should be approximately 4 to 5 feet long before being introduced into breeding projects.

4) Cycling

Cycling is a technique used to breed many snake species. Cycling refers to establishing a yearly temperature cycle featuring a transition from warm temperatures in the spring, summer and autumn, to slightly cooler temperatures in the winter. For many snake species, cycling is necessary for successful breeding.

However, green tree python breeders employ a variety of different techniques to achieve success. Some breeders employ typical cycling patterns, while others use only mild cycling strategies. Other breeders avoid cycling their snakes at all.

118

It does not appear that cycling is always necessary for green tree pythons, but cycling is an important part of the process for most experienced and successful breeders.

It is important to realize that subtle changes likely occur throughout the year, despite a breeder's attempts to keep the conditions consistent.

Those keepers who do cycle their animals usually drop the nighttime temperatures, allowing them to fall into the low 70s or high 60s. During the day, the temperatures are kept in the normal range. This is because tropical snakes must have an opportunity to raise their body temperature to avoid becoming ill.

Keepers usually cycle their snakes for one to two months before introducing the pair to each other.

5) Pairing

Because female green tree pythons should be disturbed as little as possible during the gestation process, it is best to place the male in the female's cage.

Observe the pair closely after placing them together to ensure that they are not acting antagonistically towards each other. It is rare for a male-female pair to fight, but if it does occur, you must separate the snakes immediately to prevent serious injuries.

Copulation rarely begins right after the male and female are introduced to each other. It usually takes several hours or days for the male to begin courting the female.

Some keepers elect to separate the male and female periodically throughout the breeding season, while others leave the males and females together until ovulation is witnessed. Both approaches have merit.

6) Eliciting Copulation

Occasionally, males fail to court and breed the female with whom they are paired. Sometimes, there is nothing that can be done to change this – some pairs are simply not compatible. However, green tree python breeders have devised a number of techniques over the years that may help encourage copulation.

Competition, especially amongst males, often improves breeding interest. While you can introduce another live chondro to the cage containing the breeding pair accomplish this, the males may engage in combat with each other. Often, placing the shed skin of another male in the cage with the pair is as effective as placing another snake in the cage, yet does not put the animals at risk.

If you do not have another male or shed skin to use (or you have tried such techniques unsuccessfully), it may be helpful to scratch the male near his spurs, back and vent area. This is thought to simulate the feeling caused by another male's spurs, which may spark his competitive instincts.

Some green tree python breeders have noticed that copulations often occur during thunderstorms. While you cannot control the weather, you can certainly take advantage of storms when they occur. If possible, open the windows to lower the barometric pressure in the room. Misting the snakes with water may also encourage breeding activity.

If you have tried every method possible to elicit breeding activity, and had no success, separate the animals and wait for one of them to shed. Place the animals back together immediately after the shed and hope for the best.

Ultimately, some pairs are just incompatible. In such cases there is little the keeper can do except try to switch animals and hope for better chemistry with a new pair.

7) Ovulation

Ovulation in pythons occurs when one or both of the snake's ovaries release all of the ova it contains. These eggs then travel to the oviducts, where they are fertilized by the waiting sperm and eventually shelled. At this point, the female is called gravid.

The movements of the ova cause a mid-body swelling in the female that can be quite dramatic in some cases. In other cases, the swelling may be subtle, causing keepers to miss the event altogether. In exceptional cases, the swelling can greatly exceed the size of the lump caused by an average meal.

Ovulation is a punctuated event; do not confuse it with the general, diffuse swelling that often occurs in breeding females. Ovulation usually lasts 6 to 48 hours, but if the ovaries ovulate sequentially, it is conceivable that the female may swell somewhat dramatically for several days.

Females often adopt unusual postures during the process, providing another clue that the snake is ovulating.

Matings that follow the ovulation of both ovaries have no effect on the fertility of the eggs. Accordingly, most breeders remove males after ovulation, if they have not done so already. Some breeders will provide gravid females with round-the-clock heat.

8) Gravid

Gravid green tree pythons often lie for extended periods under their heat lamps. They may even lie on their sides, directing their lateral or ventral sides up towards the heat lamp.

Some keepers feed their gravid female once or twice while they are gravid, while others cease feeding once introductions begin. If you decide to feed the female, be sure to offer smaller meals than normal, to prevent damaging the eggs.

Females typically shed once between the times of ovulation and egg deposition. Egg deposition usually occurs about 30 days after the completion of the shed cycle.

Provide the female with a suitable egg-deposition chamber when she begins entering the post-ovulation shed cycle. The egg-deposition chamber need not be elaborate, and should contain a substrate, such as dry moss or newspaper. A plastic storage box with an entrance cut into the lid makes a suitable egg-deposition chamber.

9) Color Changes

Interestingly, some green tree python females change color during reproductive cycling. The snakes, which gradually develop a pale blue wash, may revert to their former colors later or keep their blue coloration for life. It is unclear why this change happens, and its occurrence is not associated with reproductive success.

10) Egg Deposition

Female green tree pythons may deposit eggs at any hour of the day. If secluded in a private egg-deposition chamber, it may be necessary to check on her regularly, to avoid missing the event.

The eggs may be adhered to each other in a tight bundle when you find them, or they may be scattered. While some keepers separate stuck eggs, the task requires considerable skill; accordingly, novices should simply leave such eggs attached.

In both cases, it is necessary to keep the eggs oriented in the same way they were when you picked them up. Mark the tops of the eggs with a graphite pencil to keep them oriented the correct way.

11) Maternal Incubation

If you decide to let your green tree python incubate her eggs, you should disturb her as little as possible. It is important to prevent the eggs from getting wet, but a high humidity should be maintained in the cage.

Check on the female and her clutch periodically, but try not to disturb her more than necessary. About 45 days into the process, you should begin checking the eggs more frequently. When they start to dent, hatching time is drawing near.

Be sure that the young will have some way to climb out of the egg chamber once they hatch. Once several of the young have hatched, you may want to consider removing the female.

12) Artificial Incubation

Most breeders elect to incubate their eggs artificially. If nothing else, doing so allows the female to begin feeding sooner than if you allow her to incubate the eggs herself.

Many keepers also feel that it is easier to manage the eggs in an incubator, rather than relying on the job. However, some females do not demonstrate coiling instincts, or do so poorly, so you should always be prepared to move the eggs to an incubator.

However, removing the eggs from the female can be a difficult job.

Often, females become extremely defensive during this time – this includes females who are typically tame, trustworthy snakes. However, some females may remain docile despite attempts to remove the eggs.

Always have a helper when trying to remove a female from her eggs. Doing so makes the process easier on both the keeper and the kept.

Begin by trying to grasp the female gently behind the head. Immediately use your other hand to stabilize the egg mass. Have your helper use both hands to contain the eggs, and slowly remove your hand from the eggs. Then begin using your free hand to unwind the female.

With patience and a firm but gentle touch, you will successfully remove her from her eggs. In some cases, it may be easier to unwind her partially, and remove the eggs while she remains in her cage.

13) Egg Incubation

To incubate the eggs artificially, you will need some type of incubator. Beginners should purchase an entry-level, commercially produced product, but advanced keepers can construct their own.

Incubators need not be elaborate to produce good results, but they must be well insulated and maintain a very consistent internal temperature. Always use a separate thermometer as a backup to the incubator's thermometer.

Most often, the eggs are placed in small egg boxes, which are in turn placed in the incubator. Virtually any small plastic boxes will suffice for containing the eggs.

Some keepers place moistened vermiculite or perlite in the egg boxes as a substrate. Other keepers suspend the eggs directly over water. Both strategies can generate success, but vermiculite offers more room for error. Moisten the vermiculite just enough so that it clumps when squeezed in the hand.

Incubate green tree python eggs between 87 and 88 degrees Fahrenheit. The humidity should be as high as possible, without causing condensation to form on or over the eggs. Eggs do require fresh air, but a few very small (1/8th inch) holes suffice.

The eggs normally hatch in about 50 days. The young do not all emerge at once and the earliest hatchlings may emerge up to 48 hours or so before the last emerge.

Do not remove hatchlings from their eggs. Doing so may cause their umbilicus to tear, opening them to infection and cutting off a vital energy source. If any emerge and are still connected to the yolk, allow it to fall off on its own.

Young green tree pythons may take hours to exit their eggs. Do not pull them out yourself – they will emerge when they are ready.

14) Neonatal Husbandry

When the young are first removed from the incubator, they can be kept in a communal habitat (a "nursery") until their first shed.

Keep the nursery simple, with a paper substrate and several small perches. Provide at least one large, but shallow, water dish. This will help increase the humidity, but will not be a drowning hazard for the young.

As the young shed their skin for the first time, they should be moved to their own cages. Provide typical husbandry for the small green tree pythons.

Begin feeding trials soon after their first shed. Many chondros may refuse food the first or second attempt, so patience is required. By contrast, others will feed with little pause at the first opportunity.

Inducing the young to feed is often considered the most challenging aspect of green tree python breeding. Many breeders have successfully paired their snakes and incubated the eggs, only to have their entire clutch die of starvation.

Over time, green tree python keepers have developed a number of tricks that help elicit feeding responses. Scent transfer techniques are the most common, and they rely on attaching a piece of lizard skin or a bird feather to the mouse to make it smell like a desired food item.

Some keepers rely instead on defensive strikes to jump-start the snakes' feeding instincts. They do this by repeatedly eliciting strikes – with luck and sufficient perseverance, the snake is eventually likely to strike the prey and constrict it.

Chapter 13: Further Reading

Never stop learning more about your new pet's natural history, biology and captive care. Doing so will help you to provide your new pet with the highest quality of life possible.

1) Books

Bookstores and online book retailers often offer a treasure trove of information that will advance your quest for knowledge. While books represent an additional cost involved in python care, you can consider it an investment in your pet's well-being. Your local library may also carry some books about pythons, which you can borrow for no charge.

University libraries are a great place for finding old, obscure or academically oriented books about pythons and snakes. You may not be allowed to borrow these books if you are not a student, but you can view and read them at the library.

Herpetology: An Introductory Biology of Amphibians and Reptiles

By Laurie J. Vitt, Janalee P. Caldwell

Academic Press, 2013

Snakes: Their Care and Keeping

Lenny Flank

Howell Book House

Understanding Reptile Parasites: A Basic Manual for Herpetoculturists & Veterinarians

By Roger Klingenberg D.V.M.

Advanced Vivarium Systems, 1997

Keeping Snakes: A Practical Guide to Caring for Unusual Pets

David Manning

Barron's Educational Series

The Art of Keeping Snakes: From the Experts at Advanced Vivarium Systems

Philippe De Vosjoli

Advanced Vivarium Systems

Snakes: Everything about Selection, Care, Nutrition, Diseases, Breeding, and Behavior

Richard D. Bartlett, Patricia Pope Bartlett

Barron's Educational Series

Infectious Diseases and Pathology of Reptiles: Color Atlas and Text

Elliott Jacobson

CRC Press

What's Wrong with My Snake?

John Rossi, Roxanne Rossi

BowTie Press

Designer Reptiles and Amphibians

Richard D. Bartlett, Patricia Bartlett

Barron's Educational Series

Boas pythons and Pythons of the World

Mark O'Shea

New Holland Publishers

Snakes: Everything about Selection, Care, Nutrition, Diseases, Breeding, and Behavior

Richard D. Bartlett, Patricia Pope Bartlett

Barron's Educational Series

Pythons: Everything about Selection, Care, Nutrition, Diseases, Breeding, and Behavior

Patricia Pope Bartlett, Ernie Wagner

Barron's Educational Series

Pythons

Patricia Bartlett, Ernie Wagner

Barron's Educational Series

Pythons of the World: Volume I: Australia

David G. Barker and Tracy M. Barker

Advanced Vivarium Systems

The More Complete Chondro: a Comprehensive Guide to the Care and Breeding of the Green Tree Python

Greg Maxwell

Eco Herpetological

A Guide to the Snakes of Papua New Guinea

Mark O'Shea

Independent Group Pty. Ltd.

2) Magazines

Reptiles Magazine

www.reptilesmagazine.com/

Covering reptiles commonly kept in captivity, green tree pythons are frequently featured in the magazine, and its online partner.

Practical Reptile Keeping

http://www.practicalreptilekeeping.co.uk/

Practical Reptile Keeping is a popular publication aimed at beginning and advanced hobbies. Topics include the care and maintenance of popular reptiles as well as information on wild reptiles.

3) Websites

With the explosion of the Internet, it is easier to find information about reptiles than it has ever been. However, this growth has cause an increase in the proliferation of both good information and bad information.

While knowledgeable breeders, keepers and academics operate some websites, others lack the same dedication and scientific rigor. Anyone with a computer and Internet connection can launch a website and say virtually anything they want about green tree pythons. Accordingly, as with all other research, consider the source of the information before making any husbandry decisions.

The Reptile Report

www.thereptilereport.com/

The Reptile Report is a news-aggregating website that accumulates interesting stories and features about reptiles from around the world.

The Vivarium and Aquarium News

www.vivariumnews.com/

The online version of the former publication, The Vivarium and Aquarium News provides in-depth coverage of different reptiles and amphibians in a captive and wild context.

4) Journals

Herpetologica

www.hljournals.org

Published by The Herpetologists' League, Herpetologica, and its companion publication, Herpetological Monographs cover all aspects of reptile and amphibian research.

Journal of Herpetology

www.ssarherps.org/

Produced by the Society for the Study of Reptiles and Amphibians, the Journal of Herpetology is a peer-reviewed publication covering a variety of reptile-related topics.

Copeia

www.asihcopeiaonline.org/

Copeia is published by the American Society of Ichthyologists and Herpetologists. A peer-reviewed journal, Copeia covers all aspects of the biology of reptiles, amphibians and fish.

Nature

www.nature.com/

Although Nature covers all aspects of the natural world, there is plenty for snake enthusiasts.

5) Supplies

Big Apple Pet Supply

http://www.bigappleherp.com

Big Apple Pet Supply carries most common husbandry equipment, including heating devices, water dishes and substrates.

LLLReptile

http://www.lllreptile.com

LLL Reptile carries a wide variety of husbandry tools, heating devices, lighting products and more.

Doctors Foster and Smith

http://www.drsfostersmith.com

Foster and Smith is a veterinarian-owned retailer that supplies husbandry-related items to pet keepers.

6) Support Organizations

The National Reptile & Amphibian Advisory Council

http://www.nraac.org/

The National Reptile & Amphibian Advisory Council seeks to educate the hobbyists, legislators and the public about reptile and amphibian related issues.

American Veterinary Medical Association

www.avma.org

The AVMA is a good place for Americans to turn if you are having trouble finding a suitable reptile veterinarian.

The World Veterinary Association

http://www.worldvet.org/

The World Veterinary Association is a good resource for finding suitable reptile veterinarians worldwide.

References

Barker, D. G. (1994). *Pythons of the World, Volume I, Australia.* Advanced Vivarium Systems.

D. Wilson, R. H. (2006). Life-history traits and ontogenetic colour change in an arboreal tropical python, Morelia viridis. *Journal of Zoology.*

David Wilson, R. H. (2007). The adaptive significance of ontogenetic colour change in a tropical python. *Biology Letters.*

Donnellan, L. H. (2003). Phylogeographic analysis of the green python, Morelia viridis, reveals cryptic diversity. *Molecular Phylogenetics and Evolution.*

F. BRISCHOUX, L. P. (2010). Insights into the adaptive significance of vertical pupil shape in snakes. *Journal of Evolutionary Biology.*

Hillman, M. (n.d.). *Morelia viridis.* Retrieved from Animal Diversity Web: http://animaldiversity.ummz.umich.edu/accounts/Morelia_viridis/

JRossi, J. R. (2006). *What's Wrong with My Snake?* BowTie Press.

Wilson, D. (2007). Foraging ecology and diet of an ambush predator: the green python. In E. H. Powell, *Biology of the Boas and Pythons.*

Wilson, H. a. (2006). Age and sex related differences in the spatial ecology of a dichromatic tropical python (Morelia viridis). *Austral Ecology.*

Index